Library of
Davidson College

THE USAGES OF THE
AMERICAN CONSTITUTION

THE USAGES OF THE

AMERICAN CONSTITUTION

BY

HERBERT W. HORWILL, M.A.
Sometime Scholar of Wadham College, Oxford

KENNIKAT PRESS/Port Washington, N.Y.

342.73
H824u

74-9936
USAGES OF THE AMERICAN CONSTITUTION

First published 1925
Reissued 1969 by Kennikat Press

Library of Congress Catalog Card No: 68-8210
SBN 8046-0216-6
Manufactured in the United States of America

TO

K. F. H.

THE MOST DISCRIMINATING OF READERS

AND

THE MOST HELPFUL OF CRITICS

PREFACE

THE welcome given to Lord Bryce's *American Commonwealth* might have been expected to encourage English writers to pursue the line of inquiry which he followed with such conspicuous success. On the contrary, during the thirty-six years since that book was first published little addition has been made by any of his fellow-countrymen to the body of literature on the American political system. Possibly the very pre-eminence of his book has had a deterrent influence. It was so obviously *hors concours* that scarcely anyone else has ventured into a field where every opportunity of contributing to an understanding of the subject seemed to have been already pre-empted.

Yet, however accurate and comprehensive Lord Bryce's study may have been, it did not cover the whole ground in adequate detail. The subject of the present volume, although full of interest to English and American readers alike, occupies only a few pages of *The American Commonwealth*. It is, indeed, singular that American research, which during recent years seems to have peered into almost every nook and cranny of the edifice of American government, has so largely ignored the part played by usage in the actual working of the Constitution. Perhaps the explanation of such an oversight is that the importance of this subject is less likely to be recognized by an American than by an Englishman, in whose mental background the constitutional significance of usage is naturally prominent.

This book has been written primarily for an English public, and American readers must therefore be asked to excuse the inclusion of some information which to them may seem quite elementary but which one cannot assume to be common knowledge on this side of the Atlantic. It is hoped that they may find compensation in the collection and presentation of many significant historical facts not mentioned in their own text-books, to say nothing of the arguments and conclusions which, if accepted, will necessarily give a new turn to the discussion of the whole question of the American Constitution.

It may be as well to add that the present

PREFACE

volume is not the product of academic reflection at a distance. The author has spent more than six years, in all, in the United States, and during the winters of 1922-23 and 1923-4 he enjoyed the advantage of observing the working of the national political machinery close at hand in the capital city itself. He takes this opportunity of expressing his obligation not only to the Library of Congress but to the Washington Public Library, whose generous practice of allowing borrowers to take home as many as five books at the same time greatly facilitates study and research.

H. W. H.

LONDON, *August*, 1925.

CONTENTS

	PAGE
I. INTRODUCTION: WHAT IS THE AMERICAN CONSTITUTION?	1
II. THE ELECTION OF THE PRESIDENT	26
III. 'ACCIDENTAL' PRESIDENTS	58
IV. THIRD PRESIDENTIAL TERMS	88
V. THE PRESIDENT'S CABINET	101
VI. THE CABINET AND CONGRESS	113
VII. APPOINTMENT AND REMOVAL	126
VIII. THE POWER OF THE PURSE	149
IX. THE RESIDENT CONGRESSMAN	160
X. MISCELLANEOUS USAGES: PUBLIC SESSIONS OF CONGRESS, THE COMBINATION OF FEDERAL AND STATE OFFICES, THE GEOGRAPHICAL DISTRIBUTION OF OFFICES, THE INTEGRITY OF THE SUPREME COURT, TITLES OF HONOUR	175
XI. CHANGES IN CONSTITUTIONAL USAGE	196
XII. THE 'SAFEGUARDS' OF THE AMERICAN CONSTITUTION	213

I

INTRODUCTION

What is the American Constitution?

IT will help the discussion of the specific subject of this book if we begin by brushing away some cobwebs. Once upon a time some unknown humorist divided constitutions into written and unwritten, and since then text-book after text-book has taken his classification seriously. The American Constitution, we are told, is an example of the former class and the English of the latter. Presumably, then, the English Constitution is transmitted orally from generation to generation, like the earliest poetry of ancient Greece. One's imagination is fascinated by visions of the Benchers of the Inner Temple doling it out to Bar students while they eat their dinners, and of the Father of the House of Commons declaiming it to attentive groups of newly-elected M.P.'s.

But the authors of our text-books have nothing like that in their minds, it seems, when they speak of written versus unwritten constitutions. They are not employing ' written ' and ' unwritten ' in the vulgar significations of those words. According to their own account of the distinction, they use ' written ' as a convenient abbreviation of ' recorded in a single document and placed out of reach of alteration by the legislature,' while ' unwritten,' in the same code, signifies ' composed of a variety of statutes, judicial decisions, and what not, and capable of being amended by ordinary legislative enactment, or even by the adoption of a new custom.' This practice is a particularly unhappy example of the employment in an esoteric sense of words that have a fixed and clear meaning in the popular mind. Every science must have its own technical vocabulary, but it is unfortunate when, for that purpose, the simple, everyday language of the common man is conscripted to this special end and diverted from its proper signification. Confusion and misunderstanding are an inevitable result.

In this instance it has become easier for writers on the subject to use the term ' unwritten constitution ' in a peculiar and unexpected sense because of the technical meaning given by the legal profession to the term ' unwritten law,' which is applied to case law, or common law, in order to distinguish it from the ' written law ' of positive enactment. The reports of judicial decisions are written, printed, and published, but nevertheless in the terminology—one is tempted to say, in the jargon—of the profession they are ' unwritten law.' But even this precedent will not justify the classification of constitutions as written and unwritten. For those who thus speak do not mean by an unwritten constitution one that consists solely of judicial decisions and traditional usages. Their typical example of it, the English Constitution, includes also certain statutes, which, in legal terminology, would be distinguished as written. The analogy, therefore, does not hold. Anyone who insists on applying to constitutions, at the risk of popular misconception of his meaning, the esoteric distinction between so-called written and unwritten law had better take a hint from the American advertisers of partly-manufactured clothing and label the English Constitution ' semi-written.'

If we wish, then, to learn the real character of the American Constitution, we get no light at all by being told that it is written, for the same thing can be said of every constitution in existence. The fact is that all constitutions are written—and printed too—as soon as anyone collects their various provisions in a book.[1]

Perhaps we shall best understand what the American Constitution really is by first considering the nature of the English Constitution. The road may seem a roundabout one, but it will bring us the sooner to our goal. And, first of all, we must be quite clear in our minds as to what we mean by a constitution. Let us see how it is defined by two writers of the highest authority, one an Englishman and the other an American. To Dicey a constitution consists of

'all rules which directly or indirectly affect the distribution or the exercise of the sovereign power in the state.'

---

[1] Lest this contention be considered the mere vagary of an iconoclastic crank, it may be worth while to mention that the antithesis of written and unwritten constitutions is definitely rejected by Bryce in his *Studies in History and Jurisprudence*, p. 126.

'Hence,' he continues, ' it includes (among other things) all rules which define the members of the sovereign power, all rules which regulate the relation of such members to each other, or which determine the mode in which the sovereign power, or the members thereof, exercise their authority.'[1]

In the same way Judge Cooley defines a constitution as ' the body of rules and maxims in accordance with which the powers of sovereignty are habitually exercised.'[2]

Let us now accept Dicey's guidance in analysing the English Constitution. The rules to which he refers include, he points out, two sets of principles or maxims of a totally distinct character :

(1) The Law of the Constitution. This consists of rules which are enforced by the courts. It is sub-divided into (*a*) rules that have been enacted by statute, and (*b*) rules derived from the mass of custom, tradition, or judge-made maxims known as the common law.

(2) The Conventions of the Constitution. These are customs, practices, maxims, or precepts which are not enforced by the courts. As examples of the Conventions of the Constitution Dicey gives the following maxims : ' The King must assent to any bill passed by the two Houses of Parliament ' ; ' When the House of Lords acts as a Court of Appeal, no peer who is not a law lord takes part in

[1] A. V. Dicey, *Introduction to the Study of the Law of the Constitution*, ed. 1915, p. 22.

[2] T. M. Cooley, *The General Principles of Constitutional Law in the United States of America*, chapter 2.

the decisions of the House'; 'Ministers resign office when they have ceased to command the confidence of the House of Commons.' These are none of them 'laws' in the true sense of the word, for, if they were broken, no court would take notice of their violation.[1]

Both (1) and (2) are equally parts of the English Constitution. The distinction between them is that the first class is a body of undoubted law, while the rules included in the second class, however important they may be and however generally observed, are not laws at all but mere usages.

With Dicey's account of the English Constitution as our model let us now attempt a similar analysis of the Constitution of the United States, keeping always in mind that the distinction between what is a constitution and what is not does not lie in the answer to such questions as whether it is difficult or easy to change, whether it is compact in a single document or scattered through a hundred, or whether it is of superior authority to other systems of political rules. The reason for differentiation lies in the matters with which it deals. The vital question determining the inclusion or exclusion of any particular law or usage is: Does this find a place within ' the body of rules and maxims in accordance with which the powers of sovereignty are habitually exercised'? If it does it is part of the Constitution.

[1] *Op. cit.* pp. 22-26, 413.

INTRODUCTION

The moment we begin to compare the English and American Constitutions we are struck by the fact that the most important part of the American Constitution is one to which there is no parallel in the English. This unique element is an instrument drawn up by the Convention of 1787 and modified by nineteen subsequent amendments. Any enactment of Congress conflicting with it is null and void. In cases of doubt the question is decided by a judgment of the Supreme Court pronounced in some concrete instance arising out of an attempt to carry the doubtful enactment into effect. It is, of course, a complete misunderstanding to suppose that the power to nullify statutes lies with the Supreme Court. It lies really with the dead hand which the sovereign people placed in control more than a hundred years ago. The function of the judges is purely interpretative and declaratory. The neglect of this distinction has led to endless confusion of thought.

Next come such statutes as fill up the gaps in the fundamental document or develop its instructions in further detail. An example is the Act of 1887 which provides how the votes cast by the electoral colleges at a Presidential election shall be counted. This class corresponds to the English (1) (a).

Then there are various rules which are distinguished from the class immediately preceding by being derived not from statutes but from the judicial decisions which are the basis of common law, and from the class which follows by being capable of

THE AMERICAN CONSTITUTION

enforcement by the courts. These correspond to the English class (1) (*b*).

Lastly, we come to those customs, practices, maxims and precepts which are not enforced by the courts, and which thus correspond to the English class (2). We might describe them by borrowing, *mutatis mutandis*, Freeman's account of the Conventions of the English Constitution.

> 'A whole code,' he says, ' of political maxims, universally acknowledged in theory, universally carried out in practice, has grown up, without leaving among the formal acts of our legislature any trace of the steps by which it grew. . . . We have now a whole system of political morality, a whole code of precepts for the guidance of public men, which will not be found in any page of either the statute or the common law, but which are in practice held hardly less sacred than any principle embodied in the Great Charter or in the Petition of Right.'[1]

The most obvious example is the understanding that Presidential Electors shall not cast their votes according to their independent judgment but shall do no more than formally ratify the results of a previous popular vote.

This account of the constituent elements of the American Constitution differs radically from that given in the text-books, which recognize nothing as part of the Constitution which is not found in the fundamental instrument of 1787 or in its subsequent amendments. But it is the only theory that fits the facts. Whatever the tradition of the schools may

[1] E. A. Freeman, *The Growth of the English Constitution*, ed. 1876, p. 112 *et seqq*.

teach, no one can have a clear and true idea of the American Constitution who does not envisage it in this fashion. If it is part of the English Constitution that the King's Speech to Parliament, nominally declaring the intentions of the monarch, shall really express the policies of the ministry, it can be no less a part of the American Constitution that the returns from the Electoral Colleges shall really express a popular choice. Just as the ministry speaks through the King, so the multitude of American citizens speaks through the Presidential Electors. To say that the election of the President by Electoral Colleges is part of the American Constitution and his election by popular vote is not, is as absurd as it would be to say that it is part of the English Constitution that the King should address a new session of Parliament in a speech, and not a part of the Constitution that his speech should be drafted by his ministers. This convention has actually a deeper and more tenacious root in the national will than the provision adopted in 1787. No one can doubt that, in the event of an attempt to turn the formal choice by the Presidential Electors into a reality, that provision of the fundamental document would be amended in record time. To say, therefore, that the choice of a President by Electoral Colleges is part of the Constitution and that his election by the people is not, is to set up in the real world a standard of values more appropriate to some country discoverable only in the atlas of Lewis Carroll.

The usual contrasts, then, between the American

and the English Constitutions are wholly mistaken. The distinction between them is not that the one is written and the other unwritten, or that the one consists of a single document while the other is a composite of many ingredients. The American Constitution has all the ingredients of the English and one more. The supposition that it is more simple and compact and definite is an utter delusion. The one difference between the two Constitutions is that the American possesses, in addition to and antecedently to the various elements of the English, one special section which is prior to all legislative enactments and is not capable of being amended by the legislature.

Many American writers have virtually recognized that the traditional account of their Constitution is erroneous, though they have not carried their discovery to its logical conclusion by giving up the terminology which misleads the popular mind. It is recognized by Woodrow Wilson when he speaks of the fundamental instrument as a ' vigorous taproot ' from which has grown ' a vast constitutional system—a system branching and expanding in statutes and judicial decisions as well as in unwritten precedent,'[1] and when he describes as ' a sacred rule of constitutional action '[2]—constitutional action, you will notice, not political action merely—the practice, observed up to his own time, of a President's communicating his message to Congress in writing

[1] W. Wilson, *Congressional Government*, introductory chapter.
[2] W. Wilson, *The State*, ed. 1904, p. 378.

INTRODUCTION

instead of orally. It is recognized by Professor J. A. Woodburn when he says:

> 'While our Constitution is generally spoken of as written, it is not entirely written. Usage has given us, in considerable measure, an unwritten Constitution. There are many instances of constitutional understandings in America, practices and precedents, having all the force of law, that have been established by usage.'[1]

(In his various writings on the subject Professor Woodburn refers frequently to the growth in America of an unwritten Constitution in addition to the written Constitution. Apart from any question as to the propriety of the words 'written' and 'unwritten,' this account of the facts is clearly unsatisfactory, for a nation cannot have two political constitutions any more than a human being can have two physical constitutions. If the usages to which he refers have any constitutional quality at all they must be a part of a single constitution, of which the instrument of 1787 is similarly only a part.) It is recognized by Professor C. A. Beard when he declares that

> 'in fact, custom forms as large an element of our Constitution as it does in the case of the English Constitution,' and that 'when viewed from the standpoint of content there is no intrinsic difference between many statutes and the provisions of the Constitution itself; and, if we regard as constitutional all that body of law relative to the fundamental organization of the three branches of the federal government—legislative, executive and judicial—then by

[1] J. A. Woodburn, *The American Republic and its Government*, 2nd ed. p. 92.

A COMMON MISCONCEPTION

far the greater portion of our constitutional law is to be found in the statutes.'[1]

It is recognized more especially by Dr. F. A. Cleveland, when he criticizes as 'wholly illogical'[2] the restricted use of the word 'constitution' to denote the single fundamental instrument agreed upon by the people of the Union or of any one of the States, and when he maintains that

> 'by every rule of logic all provisions apportioning the exercise of sovereign powers, directing to what persons these powers are to be confined and the manner in which they are to be regulated, are equally constitutional provisions, whether found in a "written instrument," in statutes, in the common law, or in the immemorial customs of an office.'

It is easy to see how the popular misconception arose. In 1789, when the instrument drawn up in 1787 was ratified by the States and came into operation, it was actually the whole of the Constitution of the United States, and was naturally so described and labelled. At that moment there could be nothing else in the Constitution. No statutes had yet been enacted to supply its omissions or to develop any of its articles in further detail. There had grown up no body of usage or tradition to supplement it or to modify its working. A constitution comprised in a single document was, by that feature alone, in striking contrast with such a constitution as that of the mother country, and its singularity in this respect

[1] C. A. Beard, *American Government and Politics*, ed. 1924, pp. 81 and 95.
[2] F. A. Cleveland, *Organized Democracy*, ed. 1913, p. 293.

remained still the subject of comment when it was no longer singular. For the instrument of 1787 ceased to be the whole of the Constitution as soon as Congress passed the first Act dealing with constitutional matters. The Law of the Constitution was from that time onwards something more than the original document, and later there grew up also those Conventions of the Constitution which will be discussed in this book. So keen, however, was the general sense of the paramount importance of the original instrument that it escaped notice that Congressional enactments and extra-legal usages, if they helped to regulate the exercise of the powers of sovereignty, were equally part of the Constitution. Accordingly the name ' Constitution ' has continued to be exclusively applied to the instrument drawn up in 1787. Once so docketed and labelled, that instrument has retained its distinctive designation and classification ever since. But the fact that it was originally described as ' the Constitution ' does not make it the whole of the American Constitution at the present day, any more than Magna Carta would have been the whole of the English Constitution at this moment if the Barons at Runnymede had happened to declare in its preamble that they did ' ordain and establish this Constitution ' for the kingdom of England.

In yet another respect the term ' constitution ' is a misnomer when applied to this particular instrument. Such an application of the word errs by excess as well as defect. The document, as it now

AN IRRELEVANT ELEMENT

stands, is not only less than the whole of the American Constitution but it also includes something that has no logical right to a place in it at all. The members of the 1787 Convention took great pains to insure their handiwork against hasty or ill-considered alteration, but they overlooked the necessity of safeguarding it also against the interpolation of irrelevant elements. They made careful provision as to the methods by which the Constitution should be amended, but set no restriction on the nature of the changes that might be introduced. This omission was unfortunate, though the dangers lurking in it remained for a long time concealed. For more than a hundred years every amendment adopted was germane to the true and original purpose of the instrument, but in 1919 there was added an article of an entirely different character. It was an article forbidding the manufacture, sale, or transportation of intoxicating liquors. Clearly such a prohibition has no more to do with the regulation of the exercise of the powers of sovereignty within the United States than with the social order of ancient Mexico. It lies altogether outside the province of a constitution. Now the Convention of 1787 interpreted its functions quite broadly. It was not working with its eyes on a dictionary definition, and it dealt with some subjects that do not appear to affect immediately the powers of sovereignty. But neither in the original document nor in the first group of amendments, commonly known as the Bill of Rights, is there anything that can be regarded in the remotest degree as a precedent for the Eighteenth Amendment. Whether Prohibition is a good thing in itself is neither here nor there. The point is that it has nothing whatever to do with the framework of national or State government. (It would have been otherwise, of course, if the amendment had simply conferred on Congress the power to enact a prohibitory law.) The incorporation of such an article in an instrument of this nature is precisely the sort of thing that in England we should call 'unconstitutional'—something that there is no law to prevent, but that one feels ought not to be done. It is a violation of a principle that is not expressly laid down in any formal document, but that good citizens regard it as their duty to observe.

But one could not say that this amendment was 'unconstitutional' in the restricted and peculiar American sense of the word. It did not conflict with any provision of the instrument drawn up in 1787. And so the Supreme Court had no option but to pronounce it regular and 'constitutional.' Many conservatively-minded Americans are highly indignant at the addition of Amendment XVIII. to the fundamental instrument, but what else could they expect? For generations the instructors of the American people on matters relating to the Constitution have been leading them on the wrong road. They have under-emphasised, to say the least, the features that make a constitution what it is, and they have produced a general impression that the essential elements of a constitution are a validity

AN AMBIGUOUS TERM

superior to that of the ordinary law and an exceptional security against amendment or repeal. It is therefore not surprising that the advocates of Prohibition should have wished to intrench their favourite reform in this paramount and impregnable position. Now that they have shown the way there can be little doubt that the opportunity will be seized by the leaders of other popular movements also. The gilt-edged security of a Constitutional Amendment will be the natural goal of any cause commanding a large enough following throughout the country to encourage the hope of its being ratified by the requisite number of State legislatures.[1]

The word 'constitution' has thus come to be an ambiguous term. Whenever the Supreme Court has to decide whether such and such a Congressional enactment is 'constitutional,' the test is its conformity to the fundamental instrument which is known as 'the Constitution.' It is to this instrument that fidelity is pledged by members of the national and State legislatures and by all executive and judicial officers when they fulfil the requirement of taking an oath to support 'this Constitution.' In the eyes of the law the meaning of the term must necessarily be thus limited, for it is so nominated in the very bond that the judges have to interpret and the officials to observe. In such matters the original instrument has, so to speak, a copyright in its tradi-

[1] It is worth noting that, long before the ratification of the Eighteenth Amendment, the people of many States had adopted the practice of including in the Fundamental Law of those States, for similar reasons, provisions that had nothing whatever to do with constitutional matters.

tional title. But if we are considering the question of constitutions not as lawyers but as students of political institutions the customary restriction of the term is altogether misleading. By this limitation we are using the word ' constitution ' in one sense when we are discussing the government of the United States and in quite another sense when we are discussing the government of any other country, or when we are instituting comparisons between the United States and any other country. We are committing an error in classification which is bound to result in confusion of thought.

Sometimes an ambiguity may cause scarcely more than a slight inconvenience. Take ' America,' for example. This proper name means one thing when we say that America was discovered by Columbus in 1492 and quite another thing when we say that America came into the war in 1917. But in practice this double use of the word rarely leads to any misunderstanding. The context is usually sufficient to indicate to which America we are referring, especially as the ambiguity of the word is popularly recognized. It is otherwise with the word ' constitution.' Here the ambiguity is commonly ignored, and its pitfall lies hidden in the path of everyone who discusses the American system of government, and especially of everyone who attempts to compare it with the political systems of other countries. Accordingly, all comparisons between the American and the English Constitution that use the term ' American Constitution ' or ' Constitution of the

United States' in the traditional sense need re-writing, however eminent their authors. They need re-writing as much as a map of the world would need re-drawing that showed no America in the Western Hemisphere outside the boundaries of the single republic that is popularly called America. The comparisons are not *in pari materia*.

But, if we are to call things by their right names, does not the necessity for revision go further? In American law-courts the specialized application of the word 'constitution' must always prevail. In the literature of political science, however, whether one is making international comparisons or discussing the government of the United States alone, the word cannot correctly be used in any other sense than that given to it in the definitions quoted above from Dicey and Cooley. If this be so, some other term must be found for the instrument which is traditionally known as the American Constitution.

How, then, may the customary terminology best be revised? That is to say, what name can we find for the fundamental instrument which will recognize its unique character and at the same time indicate that it is not the whole of the American Constitution? Dr. F. A. Cleveland, although quite pessimistic as to the possibility of ever inducing Americans to 'change the labels' that have been put upon the fundamental documents of the Union and the several States, has suggested that, if a change were to be made, the term 'charter' would be 'entirely consistent with our conception of popular sovereignty.'

H.A.C.

That is undoubtedly true, but, while the propriety of this term would be obvious to the historian, its use would be likely to lead to further misconception by ' the man in the street.' Moreover, what we are looking for is a term that will indicate on the face of it that the document in question is part of the Constitution. ' Organic Law ' will not serve, for that is simply a synonym for ' Law of the Constitution ' and thus covers too large an area. ' The Constitution of 1787 ' (or of 1789, if we prefer to date it from the year of ratification) would answer the purpose but for the fact that a considerable part of the document as it exists to-day was not the work of the Convention of 1787. About one third of the total document is of later date, and various amendments have made so many additions to the original that the use of such a term would sometimes be an absurd anachronism. It would be ridiculous, for instance, to speak of woman suffrage as part of the Constitution of 1787.

Our quest for the term we are seeking must start, I think, from the fact that the instrument, in the form in which it is now operative, is part of that first section of the entire present-day Constitution which may be called the Law of the Constitution, as distinct from its Conventions. We now want to find some means of marking it off from the other parts of that section, *i.e.*, from statute law and common law. It will not do to call it the Supreme Law of the Constitution, for Article VI. plainly declares that all Acts of Congress passed in conformity with it, as

THE FUNDAMENTAL LAW

well as all treaties, share with it the title of 'the supreme law of the land.' If careful attention were paid to Article VI. we should not hear so much loose talk about the 'supremacy' of this instrument over Acts of Congress—about its superior validity, its greater authority, and so on. All this is not only unwarranted by the text itself, but is in actual contradiction of it. The Sherman Act is as much the supreme law of the land as the Commerce Clause. It is equally valid and equally authoritative. The practical advantage possessed by the Commerce Clause is that it has what insurance companies would call a better expectation of life. Owing to the obstacles placed in the way of its repeal it has a greater chance of longevity. But the Sherman Act, as long as it lives, is no whit inferior to it in authority or validity. It is equally a part of the supreme law of the land.

The distinction of the instrument known as the Constitution is not that it is above the ordinary law but that it is under it. It is fundamental. It is the basis of the whole legal structure of Acts of Congress and judicial decisions. This points the way to the solution of our problem. Why not call it the Fundamental Law of the Constitution? That nomenclature avoids all risk of misconception. It indicates precisely the place that this instrument occupies to-day, and always will occupy, in the Constitution as a whole, without in the least impairing its dignity or weakening the popular respect which it justly deserves. In fifty years' time, whatever amendments may have been adopted in the interval, whatever new enactments may have been placed on the statute-book, whatever additions may have been made to the body of common law, and whatever new conventions may have acquired the status of established usage, 'the Fundamental Law of the Constitution' will be as unambiguous, as precise, and as appropriate a term as it is to-day.

Perhaps it may be as well to anticipate a possible objection. Some parts of the instrument in its present-day form are later, chronologically, than many statutes, and how, it may be asked, can you speak of an amendment adopted in 1920 as fundamental while you classify an Act passed in 1820 as not fundamental? The metaphor from buildings will not, perhaps, apply perfectly, but this objection is not really very serious. Most of the amendments are in the nature not of alterations of previously existing articles, but of additions to them. We have therefore to picture to ourselves a building which is being enlarged from time to time by the construction of annexes (constitutional amendments and the consequent statutes) as well as additional stories (statutes). And the foundation of Annex B is none the less a foundation because it is of later date than some of the stories of Annex A or of the original building.

In order, then, to avoid all ambiguity and misconception, I propose to denote the fundamental instrument by the term ' The Fundamental Law of

'CONVENTIONS' 21

the Constitution,' or, for the sake of brevity, 'The Fundamental Law.'

To sum up: We have found that the American Constitution is composed of:

(1) The Law of the Constitution, comprising
   (a) The Fundamental Law of the Constitution, consisting of the Constitution of 1787 as subsequently amended (but minus Amendment XVIII.).
   (b) The Statute Law of the Constitution.
   (c) The Common Law of the Constitution.
(2) The Conventions of the Constitution.

It is of these Conventions that the present volume will treat. Its proper title would accordingly be 'The Conventions of the American Constitution.' Unfortunately, the term 'constitutional convention' has already been pre-empted in America in such fashion that the use of this title would probably be confusing. The body which drew up the Constitution of 1787 is described as a 'constitutional convention,' and the same term is normally applied to the assemblies that have been called to draft or amend the fundamental laws of the various States. The literature of the American Constitution includes a book by John Alexander Jameson, entitled *A Treatise on Constitutional Conventions*, which gives an account of the 'history, powers and modes of proceeding' of constitutional conventions in this sense of the term. Another volume covering the same ground has been written by Mr. Roger Sherman Hoar, with the title *Constitutional Conventions : their Nature, Powers, and Limitations*. Both librarians and students would have reason to complain of the publication of a book bearing a title so similar to those of Judge Jameson's and Mr. Hoar's but occupied with an entirely different subject. The present writer has therefore reluctantly decided to adopt the title *The Usages of the American Constitution*—reluctantly, because the word 'usage' does not express the leading idea as precisely as 'convention.' A 'usage' is merely a customary or habitual practice; a 'convention' is a practice that is established by general tacit consent. 'Usage' denotes something that people are accustomed to do; 'convention' indicates that they are accustomed to do it because of a general agreement that it is the proper thing to do. There is no help for it, however, and the author, in sending out this volume with the title that it bears, can only ask his readers to bear in mind throughout that the usages of which it speaks are really practices which would be accurately described as conventions.

No document in the world, outside Holy Writ, has been the occasion of such a mass of annotation and exposition as the Fundamental Law of the American Constitution. It has been examined as critically and minutely as though it were believed to be verbally inspired. The two other sections of the Law of the Constitution—at any rate, as they were thirty years ago—have been dealt with by Professor

A GAP TO BE FILLED

C. G. Tideman in *The Unwritten Constitution of the United States*, published in 1890, which has for its thesis :

> 'The Federal Constitution contains only a declaration of the fundamental and most general principles of constitutional law, while the real living constitutional law—that which the people are made to feel around and about them, controlling the exercise of power by government and protecting the minority from the tyranny of the majority—the flesh and blood of the Constitution, instead of its skeleton, is here, as elsewhere, unwritten ; not to be found in the instrument promulgated by a constitutional convention, but in the decisions of the courts and acts of the legislature, which are published and enacted in the enforcement of the written Constitution.'

And, of course, there are many more recent treatises on statutes and common law, which, although not formally published as accounts of the non-fundamental sections of the Law of the Constitution, supply the student with all the information he can need concerning them.

The Law of the Constitution, then, has been adequately looked after. But, as far as I can discover, no one has yet attempted to discuss the Usages of the Constitution as a specific subject. Incidental references to particular Usages may be found scattered here and there in many books on American government, but the importance of this section of the Constitution has not been sufficiently recognized to suggest the compilation of a volume devoted entirely to it. It is this deficiency that the present writer hopes in some measure to supply in the following pages. He does not suppose for a moment that he has given a complete and exhaustive account of the subject. He is breaking new ground, and his work must therefore suffer from the imperfections that beset the labours of the pioneer. This volume, however, will have served a useful purpose if it arouses attention to the importance of the subject and stimulates some better-equipped explorer to continue the trail that the present writer has blazed.

It will be noticed that some of the Usages discussed in this book have been treated at much greater length than others. While symmetry is often a desirable aim, it has seemed inexpedient in this instance to follow the example of Procrustes. Some of these Usages are so familiar as to require little attention, while others—not always, perhaps, more important in themselves—needed a fuller exposition.

When both the Law and the Usages of the Constitution have been adequately expounded the opportunity will come for some one to do for the American Constitution what Bagehot did for the English. The existing books purporting to deal with the American Constitution concern themselves with the Fundamental Law only, and are accordingly too limited in their scope to meet the need. On the other hand, the many excellent accounts that have been written of the American political system cover too large an area. They include discussions of many political topics that are outside the framework of the national government. Bagehot did not think it necessary to consider the organization of political

AN AMERICAN BAGEHOT

parties or the methods of municipalities in the appointment of their officials, and an American Bagehot will similarly confine himself to such matters as fall definitely within the boundaries of the Constitution.

II

THE ELECTION OF THE PRESIDENT

ONE of the principal aims of the founders of the American Republic was to make the New World safe against democracy. Many of them would have been inexpressibly shocked if they had been told that they were establishing a system of government of the people, by the people, and for the people. 'The Constitution,' as Mr. Herbert Croly has aptly said, 'was the expression not only of a political faith, but also of political fears.' Indeed, the very object of calling the Convention of 1787 was largely to secure a more efficient government for the protection of the rights of property, and some of its most prominent members made no secret of their conservative attitude. 'The people,' declared Roger Sherman in one of the debates, 'should have as little to do as may be with the government.'

> 'Pure democracies,' wrote Madison, 'have ever been spectacles of turbulence and contention, have ever been found incompatible with personal security or the rights of property, and have in general been as short in their lives as they have been violent in their deaths.' [1]

America had shaken off the yoke against which she had made such vehement protest in the Declaration

[1] *The Federalist*, No. 10.

SAFE AGAINST DEMOCRACY

of Independence, and her leaders were in no mind to substitute the tyranny of a sovereign people for that of a sovereign monarch.

'The federal government,' says Woodrow Wilson, 'was not by intention a democratic government. In plan and structure it had been meant to check the sweep and power of popular majorities. ... The government had, in fact, been originated and organized upon the initiative and primarily in the interest of the mercantile and wealthy classes.'[1]

Conservatives like Senator Lodge and radicals like Walter E. Weyl agree in emphasizing the care taken by the framers of the Constitution of 1787 to prevent domination by the multitude.[2] Not only by making the amendment of that instrument so difficult, but by devising checks and balances on the three separate powers of the government, by giving the federal judges a life tenure, by creating a Senate invested with peculiar authority, and especially by preventing the choice of the President by popular vote, they did their best, as Weyl puts it, to bottle up popular rights for all time.

Their anxiety to safeguard the Presidency against the dangers they conceived to be involved in a direct election is the more remarkable because at that time the elective franchise, even for the State Legislatures, was in most States limited by property and other qualifications. It is estimated that, out of

[1] W. Wilson, *Division and Reunion*, ed. 1902, p. 12. For a brilliant and detailed exposition of this statement see C. A. Beard, *An Economic Interpretation of the Constitution of the United States*.

[2] See Henry Cabot Lodge, *The Senate of the United States*, ed. 1921, p. 15, and Walter E. Weyl, *The New Democracy*, ed. 1912, p. 13.

the 4,000,000 inhabitants of the thirteen colonies, there were only 150,000 persons qualified to vote.[1] At that rate one might have supposed that there was little danger of respectable citizens being swamped by the mass of what we should now call the proletariat. However, whether their apprehensions were well grounded or not, the members of the Convention were determined to be on the safe side. ' It would be as unnatural,' said one of them, ' to refer the choice of a proper person for President to the people as to refer a trial of colours to a blind man.' Another believed that ' the people would never be sufficiently informed of the character of men to vote intelligently for the candidates that might be presented.' The member who first suggested direct popular election to the office introduced his proposal with the half-apologetic statement that he was almost unwilling to declare the mode of selection he preferred, ' being apprehensive that it might appear chimerical.'[2]

The method finally devised was that of an indirect election—in certain contingencies, a doubly and even trebly indirect election. Each State was to appoint, in such manner as its Legislature might direct, a number of Electors equal to the whole number of the Senators and Representatives it sent to Congress. No Senator or Representative, or person holding an office of trust or profit under the

[1] See W. H. Taft, *Popular Government*, ed. 1913, p. 13.
[2] See J. H. Dougherty, *The Electoral System of the United States*, p. 13, and Grover Cleveland, *Presidential Problems*, p. 8.

THE ORIGINAL SCHEME   29

United States was to be eligible for appointment. The Electors were to meet in their respective States on the same day and vote by ballot for two persons, one of whom, at least, should not be an inhabitant of the same State with themselves. Their independence was safeguarded by the provision that they should vote by ballot. The votes were then to be sent to the seat of government to be counted. The person found to have the greatest number of votes was to be the President, and the next on the list the Vice-President. By an amendment adopted in 1804 the original plan was henceforth modified so that the Electors were to vote separately for President and Vice-President, and the distinct lists of the voting for each office would then be sent to the national capital.

At this point the description of the system usually stops short. But an essential feature of the scheme has yet to be mentioned. It was further provided, according to the plan of 1787, that, if no one obtained a majority of the whole number of Electors, the House of Representatives should choose the President by ballot from the five highest on the list; and, according to the plan of 1804, that, in a similar event, the House should choose him from the three highest. This supplementary provision has commonly been ignored or, at best, lightly regarded by writers on the subject. It has been so little known that, in the election campaign of 1924, when there appeared a prospect of its being needed and utilized, the discovery of the existence of such a provision occasioned general surprise. There was even a widespread feeling that those whose action, in nominating a third ' ticket,' seemed likely to occasion this result were violating the spirit of the Fundamental Law. The indifference of writers on the Constitution to this provision is presumably to be explained by the fact that only twice in the history of the United States has it become operative, and that the latest instance occurred as long as a hundred years ago. The rarity of its use is quite irrelevant, however, to the question of the nature of the original plan, and the text-books have no excuse for paying so little attention to it. The men who framed this provision believed that it would form part of the normal method of election. As the Electors would not confer together in a single assembly, but would cast their votes by ballot in their several States according to their individual judgment, it was natural to expect that—as soon as George Washington was no longer available for the supreme position—the voting would be so scattered as not to give a majority to any one person.

> ' The Convention acted on the assumption that this would happen in the great majority of cases. " Nineteen times in twenty " Mason asserted in the Federal Convention, and a little later in the Virginia State Convention he claimed forty-nine times out of fifty the vote of the Electors would not be decisive.' [1]

[1] Max Farrand, *The Framing of the Constitution of the United States*, ed. 1913, p. 166 *et seqq.* Professor Farrand seems to be the only modern writer on the subject who realizes the importance of this feature of the scheme.

DOUBLY OR TREBLY INDIRECT

We find, too, that Hamilton gave great weight to this supplementary provision. In No. 66 of the *Federalist* he mentions the power thus given to the House as one of the ' important counterpoises ' provided by the Constitution of 1787 to the authority of the Senate in trying impeachments. The House, he points out,

> ' will be the umpire in all elections of the President which do not unite the suffrages of a majority of the whole number of the Electors, a case which it cannot be doubted will sometimes, if not frequently, happen.'
> ' The constant possibility of the thing,' argues Hamilton, ' must be a fruitful source of influence to that body. The more it is contemplated, the more important will appear this ultimate though contingent power, of deciding the competitions of the most illustrious citizens of the Union, for the first office in it. It would not perhaps be rash to predict that as a means of influence it will be found to outweigh all the peculiar attributes of the Senate.'

Again, Madison, in No. 39 of the *Federalist*, refers to ' the immediate election ' of the President by the States and his ' eventual election ' by the House of Representatives as showing that ' the executive power will be derived from a very compound source.'

The election of the President, then, would always be indirect. It would be doubly indirect if the members of the Electoral Colleges were not chosen by popular vote but were appointed by the State Legislatures or otherwise. And it would be trebly indirect if, as was expected to occur frequently, the voting in the Electoral Colleges virtually amounted to no more than a nomination of five (or, later, three)

32 THE ELECTION OF THE PRESIDENT

picked candidates among whom the House of Representatives would make the decisive choice.

The members of the Convention of 1787 congratulated themselves that, whatever flaws might be found elsewhere in the instrument they had drawn up, here at any rate they had hit upon something that would triumphantly meet any test.

> 'The mode of the appointment of the Chief Magistrate of the United States,' wrote Hamilton, ' is almost the only part of the system of any consequence which has escaped without severe censure or which has received the slightest mark of approbation from its opponents.'[1] The ' immediate election,' he pointed out, would be ' made by men most capable of analyzing the qualities adapted to the station and acting under circumstances favourable to deliberation and to a judicious combination of all the reasons and inducements that were proper to govern their choice.' Moreover, ' the precautions which have been so happily concerted in the system under consideration promise an effectual security against this mischief [the danger of tumult and disorder]. The choice of several to form an intermediate body of Electors will be much less apt to convulse the community with any extraordinary or violent movements than the choice of one who was himself to be the final object of the public wishes. And as the Electors chosen in each State are to assemble and vote in the State in which they are chosen, this detached and divided situation will expose them much less to heats and ferments which will be communicated from them to the people than if they were all to be convened at one time in one place.'

Now let us see what has happened. The method

[1] *The Federalist*, No. 67.

THE SCHEME NULLIFIED

prescribed by the Fundamental Law of the Constitution is still followed in every detail, but there have been established two usages, the combined result of which is to nullify the whole scheme and to bring about the very thing that those who framed it were most anxious to avoid. One of them makes it imperative for the State Legislatures to direct that the appointment of Presidential Electors shall be made by popular vote. The other has transformed the independent Electors into mere clerks who formally record a choice already made by the same vote.

First, let us consider the method of the appointment of Electors.[1] 'Each State shall appoint, in such manner as the Legislature thereof may direct,' runs the Fundamental Law. There might therefore be to-day—supposing that human ingenuity could contrive so many plans—no less than forty-eight different ways in which Electors might be chosen. There is nothing, technically, to prevent a State Legislature from choosing its Electors by its own vote, or from placing the responsibility of selecting them upon the Governor of the State. The Legislature of New York might decide, if it pleased, that the Electors of that State should be chosen by competitive examination from among the 'district leaders' of Tammany Hall. Actually there was at first a great diversity in the methods adopted. At several of the early Presidential elections the Electors

[1] Fuller particulars of the various methods adopted by different States from time to time may be found in J. H. Dougherty's *The Electoral System of the United States*, E. Stanwood's *History of the Presidency*, and A. K. McClure's *Our Presidents and how we make them*.

in the majority of the States were appointed by the State Legislatures themselves. South Carolina did not abandon this practice until 1868. Colorado, on being admitted to the Union in 1876, adopted this plan at her first election in the same year, presumably because there was not time for the newly-organized State to make the arrangements necessary for the more popular method. Long before 1868, however, it had become the general custom for the choice to be made by popular vote, though for many years there were sharp controversies as to whether the election should be made ' by general ticket,' *i.e.* by a mass vote of the whole State, or ' by districts.' The point is a highly important one, especially in the case of a State which has a large population and therefore a large Electoral College. New York, for instance, was entitled to forty-five Electors in 1924. On the general ticket system all these Electors were Republicans, whereas if the district system had been employed several of them would have been Democrats. Obviously the district system gives a much better chance for the representation of minorities, but the general system is now universally adopted. An indirect result is that it promotes the concentration of electioneering efforts upon the larger States.

For nearly half a century, then, in every State, and for a full century in nearly all the States, the Presidential Electors have been chosen by popular vote. That method of selecting them is now taken as a matter of course, and to-day no member of a

'APPOINTING' THE ELECTORS

State legislature in any part of the Union would risk his political life by advocating any other plan. The prevailing usage is firmly established in the national system of government. But such a democratic practice was never for a moment contemplated by the framers of the Fundamental Law.

> 'There was certainly no intention,' says Professor J. W. Burgess, 'of making the appointment of Presidential Electors subject to popular election. I think it is evident that the framers were anxious to avoid this. The well-known fact that in several of the commonwealths the legislatures chose the Presidential Electors at the first election and for a considerable period afterwards is certainly good evidence of the general opinion of the meaning of the phrase " Each State shall appoint ".'[1]

The growth of this unanticipated usage would not in itself have so seriously changed the character of the Presidential election if another usage had not at the same time revolutionized the function of the Presidential Electors. Here, as in the method of choosing the Electors, the provisions of the Fundamental Law, as summarized above, are strictly carried out, as well as a subsequent instruction that 'the Congress may determine the time of choosing the Electors and the day on which they shall give their votes; which day shall be the same throughout the United States.' (The time of choosing the Electors is now fixed by statute as the Tuesday next after the first Monday in November, and the day on which they shall give their votes as the second

[1] J. W. Burgess, *Political Science and Constitutional Law*, ed. 1891, vol. ii. p. 219.

Monday in the January following.) But the independence of the Electors has completely disappeared. They are themselves the nominees of a party which has instructed them in advance as to the persons for whom they are to vote. They meet in January, not to exercise their minds on the problem of the fittest man to go to the White House, but to carry out a popular mandate. Their responsibility means as little nowadays as the *congé d'élire* addressed to an English cathedral chapter.

It is commonly stated that the Presidential Electors take no definite pledge to support the nominee of their party, and that their obligation to vote for him rests, therefore, upon no more than an honourable understanding. But there is at least one State in which they are rigidly bound to do so. In Oregon it is prescribed by law that the party candidates for Electorships ' shall pledge themselves, if elected, to vote for their party nominee for President and Vice-President of the United States in the Electoral College.' (This is one of many examples of the extraordinary American practice of regulating party affairs by statute—a practice which extends in many States even to such matters as the election of local party committees and the appointment of local representatives on the national party committee.) In Pennsylvania the ' regularity ' of Electors is ensured by the curious legal provision that

> ' the nominee of each political party for the office of President of the United States shall, within thirty days after his nomination by the national convention, nominate as

PARTY 'REGULARITY'

many persons to be the candidates of his party for the office of Presidential Elector as the State is then entitled to.'

These names are to be certified by the Presidential nominee to the Secretary of the Commonwealth. Any vacancies that may subsequently occur on the list are also to be filled by the Presidential nominee. Here we find the original plan not only thwarted but turned topsy-turvy. Instead of the Electors choosing the President, they are to owe their own appointment to selection by a Presidential nominee! In other States the nominations to Electorships are variously made by State or district party conventions. Whether an Elector knows, before he accepts a nomination to the office, whom he will be expected to support, depends on the date of these conventions, some of which are held before and others after the national convention at which the Presidential candidate is selected.

The lack of a formal pledge does not really leave any freedom of choice to the Electors. There has been no instance within living memory of any failure to obey the party's behests, but everyone is agreed that, if such a thing happened, the culprit, however technically innocent of any violation of the law, would suffer severe penalties. According to Professor J. A. Woodburn, any Presidential Elector who voted independently for a candidate of his own choice

> ' would probably not find it comfortable to return home.'
> He ' would be ostracized and despised and would be

visited with the social condemnation and contempt due to one who had been guilty of an infamous betrayal of a public trust ; and a Presidential candidate elected by such betrayal would probably not accept the office.'[1]

Benjamin Harrison, indeed, goes so far as to predict that ' an Elector who failed to vote for the nominee of his party would be the object of execration, and in times of very high excitement might be the subject of a lynching.'[2]

The loss of all freedom of choice by the Electors is openly recognized in the very form of the ballot paper used at the November election. The typical American ballot paper is radically different from the English. The names of the candidates for the various offices to be filled are arranged according to parties in parallel columns, under the headings 'Republican Ticket,' 'Democratic Ticket,' 'Socialist Ticket,' and so on, with a final ' Blank Column ' in which an eccentric voter may write any other names he pleases. At the head of the list of the nominees of each several party for the Electoral College are printed the names of the candidates for the Presidency and the Vice-Presidency whom these men will support if chosen as Electors. As a matter of fact, most voters enter the polling booth without being aware of the names of the persons their party has nominated as Electors, but the printing of the party heading, with the appended names of the Presidential

[1] J. A. Woodburn, *The American Republic and its Government*, ed. 1916, p. 122.

[2] B. Harrison, *This Country of Ours*, ed. 1898, p. 77.

THE ELECTORAL MEETINGS

and Vice-Presidential candidates, is a sufficient guide for the correct casting of the vote.

Accordingly, as soon as the votes at the popular election in November have been counted, it is known for a certainty how the voting will go in the Electoral Colleges in January. On the prescribed day in the New Year more than five hundred highly respectable gentlemen will take the trouble to journey to the capitals of their respective States, will take an oath to be faithful to the Constitution whose intention they are about to violate, and will solemnly go through all the motions of casting secret ballots inscribed with the names of the persons whom their party has instructed them to support. If Hamilton were alive to watch the process he would certainly be satisfied that the actual election is still free from the ' heats and ferments ' which he was so anxious to prevent.

How completely the choice by the Electors has been reduced to a formality is indicated by the universal practice to-day in the dating of Presidential elections. Up to the passing of the Act of 1887 which regulated the electoral counting, the Electors met in the December following the November of the popular election. Although they now meet in January, and therefore in a different year, everybody dates the Presidential elections from the year in which the popular vote was cast. We say, for instance, that Mr. Harding was elected President in 1920. Strictly speaking, there was no Presidential election in that year. All that took place then was the election of the Electors, and Mr. Harding was not elected until these Electors met to cast their ballots for him in January, 1921. But it would be considered sheer pedantry to date his election otherwise than on November 2, 1920.

Professor Dicey does not exaggerate when he declares that ' the power of an Elector to elect is as completely abolished by constitutional understandings in America as is the royal right of dissent from bills passed by both Houses by the same force in England.'[1] For an American account of the transformation it is sufficient to quote Woodrow Wilson in the chapter on ' The Executive ' in his *Congressional Government.*

> ' Once,' he says, ' the functions of a Presidential Elector were very august. He was to speak for the people; they were to accept his judgment as theirs. He was to be as eminent in the qualities which win trust as was the greatest of the Imperial Electors in the power which inspires fear. But now he is merely a registering machine —a sort of bell-punch to the hand of his party convention. It gives the pressure, and he rings. It is, therefore, patent to everyone that that portion of the Constitution which prescribes his functions is as though it were not.'

Mr. Wilson's metaphor of the bell-punch is one of so many disparaging comparisons scattered through the literature of the subject that one is left somewhat surprised that any man of reputation should be willing to accept an office that is so contemptuously spoken of. The Presidential Electors are ' a mere cog-wheel in the machine ' (Bryce), ' mere ornamental figure-heads ' (Von Holst), ' a body of

[1] A. V. Dicey, *Law of the Constitution*, 8th ed. p. 29.

A MERE FORMALITY

political dummies' (A. D. Sedgwick), 'animated rubber stamps' (ex-Vice-President Marshall), or like 'the marionettes in a Punch and Judy show' (Senator Ingalls). Two Judges of the Supreme Court (Miller and Bradley) have called them 'puppets.' Perhaps the most unkindest cut of all is Professor J. Franklin Jameson's analogy from physiology.

> 'The Electoral College,' he remarks, 'has become an obsolete organ, which either avails nothing or avails occasionally to disturb and pervert the function which it was originally designed to subserve, like that singular result of evolution, the appendix vermiformis, whose only present office is occasionally by obstruction to produce acute peritonitis.'[1]

Was there ever a more singular example of the vanity of human wishes and plans? Party combinations were the evil which the framers of the Fundamental Law especially dreaded in the election of the President, and against which they took the most careful precautions. In almost every detail of their scheme they kept this purpose in view. This was the main reason for providing that the Electors should meet in separate State Colleges instead of in a single national College, that they should cast their votes in all the different States on the same day, and that they should be permitted to make but one attempt at a choice.[2] The fear of party combina-

---

[1] J. F. Jameson, *Introduction to the Study of the Constitutional and Political History of the States*, ed. 1886, p. 13.

[2] See a speech given by Rufus King in the Senate on March 18, 1824, and quoted in Professor Max Farrand's *Records of the Federal Convention of 1787*, vol. iii. p. 462.

tions also prompted the instruction that, if the counting of Electoral votes in Congress showed that there was a tie or that no candidate had a majority of the whole number of Electors, the House of Representatives should 'immediately' choose a President. Actually the process of the election of an American President offers, on a larger scale than anything else in the world, the spectacle of the domination of public life by party organizations. Every year, on Washington's birthday, it is the custom to read in each house of Congress the farewell address in which he so earnestly denounced party combinations as one of the greatest menaces to the welfare and even to the stability of the new republic. This annual programme has become so much a matter of course that no one seems to appreciate the irony of such a celebration of the day. Perhaps the grotesqueness of the juxtaposition would be more evident if the address were read at the opening session of every national nominating convention.

One might naturally suppose that the practical supersession of the Electoral Colleges must have been due to popular pressure; that at some time or other the multitude of American citizens must have insisted on having a President who was the man of their own choice. That, however, is not what happened. The Electors had actually lost their independence long before they had themselves come to be chosen by the people; that is, while they were still, in most of the States, appointed by the State Legislature. It was not any demand for popular control but the intensity of party rivalry that reduced the Electors to nonentities. The result of the first two elections, those of 1789 and 1792, was a foregone conclusion. On each occasion George Washington was elected unanimously. He would have been chosen just as surely whatever system of election had been adopted. In 1796 the Electors still exercised an unfettered independence. Before 1800, however, party organization had begun to intervene in its own interests. The Federalist members of Congress, coming together in a ' caucus ' or party meeting, took the liberty of recommending candidates for the Presidency and Vice-Presidency, and their example was followed by the Anti-Federalists, or Republicans. The members of the Anti-Federalist caucus were modest enough in offering their services. In making their recommendation they had acted, they said,

> ' only in their individual character as citizens '; they had been ' induced to adopt this measure from the necessity of the case ; from a deep conviction of the importance of union to Republicans throughout all parts of the United States in the present crisis of both our external and internal affairs, and as being the most practicable mode of consulting and respecting the interests and wishes of all upon a subject so truly interesting to the whole people of the United States.'

The Congressmen had to depend upon their personal influence with Electors to secure the adoption of their nominations, and, although not every Elector was willing to accept dictation of this kind, they were, on the whole, successful. They were the acknowledged leaders of the respective parties, and their preferences, as such, were bound to carry weight. At this stage the authority of the Congressional caucuses was greatly reinforced by the constitutional provision that the Electors should meet in separate State groups instead of in a single body. This provision, deliberately adopted by the Convention of 1787 for the purpose of preventing cabals, deprived the Electors of all opportunity of mutual consultation. It was, of course, not necessary to the efficient working of the scheme, as originally intended, that there should be any mutual consultation at all, even among the Electors of a single State. If the votes cast throughout the country were scattered, there was the House of Representatives to make the final decision. But the moment that the triumph of a party became an object of ambition, it was essential that the representatives of that party in the Electoral Colleges should speak with a single voice. The Federalists might be in a majority throughout the country, but if the Federalists in Massachussetts voted for one man and the Federalists in Pennsylvania for another, while the Anti-Federalists in all the States concentrated their votes on a single candidate, an Anti-Federalist would be likely to become President. Neither party could afford to overlook the importance of having some central organization, of acknowledged authority, which would thrash out all competing claims before the Electors met and would present to those Electors who wished to be loyal to the party

THE CAUCUS METHOD 45

a 'ticket' for their adoption. Such an organization offered itself in the Congressional party caucus. The experiment of 1800 was so successful that it was repeated at following elections, though the disappearance of the Federalists from the political scene left only one party to hold a caucus until a new division of parties developed itself. The Republican caucus felt it none the less necessary to continue in being meanwhile, and to make its nominations every four years, in order to retain its hold upon the Presidential office. During this period nominations were also made from time to time by various State legislatures, as well as by occasional mass meetings of party adherents, but the greater influence was naturally exercised by the Congressional caucuses.

The last Congressional caucus for the nomination of a Presidential candidate was held in 1824. It is significant that this date approximately synchronises with the period when the method of choosing Electors by popular vote, instead of appointing them by the State Legislatures, had become generally adopted. By this time there had grown up a strong democratic spirit, which resented the authority of the Congressional caucus as a usurpation—not of the functions of the Electors but of the rights of the people. The caucus method, while it lasted, had indirectly strengthened the House of Representatives at the expense of the Senate, which, being the smaller body, contributed fewer members to the joint caucus of both chambers. The authority wielded by the House in determining who should be nominated gave it also an inordinate influence on general politics. Madison, for instance, had to accept the policies dictated to him by the leaders of the House as a condition of his re-election. In 1828 the place of a Congressional caucus was taken by similar caucuses in the legislatures of several States, at the obvious risk of failure to secure unity of choice. In 1832 there was introduced the system which has held its ground ever since—the nomination of candidates for the Presidency and Vice-Presidency by party national conventions, composed of delegates sent by conventions of the same party in the several States. A national convention is obviously more fully representative than a Congressional caucus could be, as it includes delegates from those States where the party is in a minority and is therefore unable to send any members to Congress.

It is impossible to fix precisely the date at which the Electors ceased to exercise an independent judgment. Perhaps the latest, and certainly the most conspicuous, instance of the casting of an unfettered vote occurred in 1820. In that year William Plumer, of New Hampshire, a former Governor of the State who had also at one time represented it in the Senate, was the only Elector who voted against Monroe's re-election. He cast his ballot for John Quincy Adams.

'He was influenced,' says his son and biographer, 'in part, perhaps, by a desire to draw attention to his friend

THE LAST FREE VOTE

Adams, whom he thus first nominated for the Presidency; but more by his disapprobation of what he regarded as the wasteful extravagance of the public expenditure during Monroe's first term of service.'[1]

His vote, we learn on the same authority, ' excited much wonder and some censure at the time.' It created, however, no surprise in those who knew him, ' as it was the natural result of his general rule of independent action, combined with his avowed opinions respecting some of the leading measures of Mr. Monroe's administration.' William Plumer, jr., who was then a member of Congress, tells us that he received many congratulations on his father's vote from Republicans of the old school, and points out that it was an anticipation of the public opinion of four years later, when Monroe retired into obscurity and Adams was chosen President. One hopes that a statue has been erected somewhere in the elder Plumer's honour. Certainly, many men have received that distinction who have deserved it much less.

In two ways, then, usage has revolutionized the original plan. It has reduced the possible variety in the appointment of Electors to the single method of a popular vote, and it has robbed the Electors of all freedom of choice. By what means the parties impose their will upon the Electors is a matter of interest, but it is of no importance as relating to the practical nullification of the Fundamental Law. The significant thing is that, whatever machinery the

[1] *Life of William Plumer*, by William Plumer, jr., ed. 1857, p. 493.

parties may employ to secure their end, the Electors do no more than register a popular vote that has already been given. The effect would be the same whether the party nominees were selected by conventions, by primary elections, or by a postal vote like the referendum on the Bok Peace Prize scheme.

Actually, the convention system has grievously disappointed those who wish the President to be really the choice of a majority of American citizens. At the November elections they can only pronounce between the nominees already selected by the several parties. And the rank and file of a party are very far from being able to select that party's candidate. Indeed, what has really been established is a system of party Electoral Colleges for the making of nominations. Through a gradation of district and State conventions the members of a party choose indirectly the members of the national convention, and these select the candidate. Of late years an attempt has been made to give everybody a voice by means of the method of direct primaries; *i.e.* the members of a party in each locality vote directly for a Presidential nominee, and the delegates to the State and national conventions are under an obligation to support this choice. This effectually brings about the selection of the candidate by the mass of the party members whenever there is immediately an absolute majority for any one man. If, however, the first vote taken at a national convention does not give anyone the requisite majority—at the Democratic convention a two-thirds majority is necessary

THE CONVENTION METHOD 49

—the convention has to vote again and again until this result is attained. (English readers, by the way, must beware of being misled by the general use of the word ' ballot ' for the vote of a convention. So far from recording their preference in secret, the delegates shout it at the top of their voices.) As soon, therefore, as the supporters of any candidate realize that their favourite has no chance, they transfer their votes, at their own discretion, to some one else, thus acting with as complete a freedom as the members of the Electoral College were intended to exercise.

It is when there appears to be a deadlock between two or three leading rivals, no one of whom can secure an absolute majority, that there comes the opportunity of the ' bosses ' to solve the problem by some adroit deal in votes. A stage has then been reached at which the delegates must forsake their ' instructions ' from home and vote according to such persuasion as may be brought to bear upon them from other sources. Mr. Harding's nomination in 1920 was practically determined by a small group of men meeting in midnight session in a bed-room of a Chicago hotel. At the first ballot he was sixth on the list, with less than seven per cent. of the total votes. At the eighth ballot his original vote was doubled, and at the tenth it was multiplied tenfold. At the Democratic convention of the same year it was not until the forty-fourth ballot that Mr. Cox secured the nomination. No one can doubt that if, at the election of November, 1920, each voter, without any previous nominations, had been given a blank ballot paper on which he was to write the name of the man he favoured for the Presidency, neither Mr. Harding nor Mr. Cox would have headed the poll. In 1924, at the Democratic convention all previous records were broken by the failure of any candidate to secure a majority until the 103rd ballot.

Thus the outraged Fundamental Law has taken its revenge. The American citizen, in his eagerness to nullify its purpose and to exercise a direct choice for the Presidency, has really done no more than remove the Electoral College system to an earlier stage of the process. For what, in effect, is the Republican National Convention but an Electoral College for the choice of a Republican candidate?

The effect of these radical changes in the method of electing the President has been far-reaching. In the first place, the type of man selected has been very different from that which would have found most favour with those groups of well-informed, thoughtful, and non-partisan citizens whom the Convention of 1787 contemplated as constituting the Electoral Colleges. There is a well-known maxim that many a man who would make an excellent President would be a poor Presidential candidate. It is the qualities of a good President rather than those of a good candidate that would have carried most weight with such unbiased and competent judges of character as the Electors were intended to be. Nine out of ten of the candidates actually nominated by the party conventions would have

IF THE CANDIDATE DIED

failed to gain their approval. Another result has been the strengthening of the power of the Presidency as against that of Congress. The Presidency would never have acquired such authority as it possesses over the Federal government to-day if it had been filled according to the original plan. A President who was not the choice of the mass of the people would not have been allowed to magnify his office at the expense of a popularly elected legislature. But, believing him to be its own creation, the country has been content that he should exercise a power which it would have denied him if he had not owed his position to the popular vote.

Is there any possibility of the Electors regaining their forfeited independence? A situation is conceivable which would put the matter to the test.

> 'Should accident so shape events,' writes Dr. Von Holst, 'that the Presidential candidate of the victorious party should die immediately before the meeting of the Electoral College, then the United States would again have a President who was, not only in form but in truth, elected by the Electors. The effects that such an accident might produce are incalculable.'[1]

Such a case has never yet occurred. The nearest approach to it was in 1872, but with the important difference that the man who died was the candidate not of the victorious but of the defeated party. Horace Greeley, who had been defeated as Democratic candidate at the popular election on November 5, died on November 29. The Electors

---

[1] H. Von Holst, *The Constitutional Law of the United States of America*, Mason's translation, ed. 1887, p. 87.

met a week later, on the very day on which he was carried to his grave. Out of a total of 366 Electoral votes there were sixty-six that would have come to him if he had lived. These sixty-six votes belonged to Democratic Electors in six States. The three Democratic Electors in Georgia evaded the difficulty by voting for the dead man. They felt themselves under a sacred obligation to vote for Greeley, and vote for him they did, although at the time he was in his coffin. The other Democratic votes were divided among four candidates, T. A. Hendricks receiving forty-two, B. Gratz Brown (the official party candidate for the Vice-Presidency) eighteen, C. J. Jenkins two, and D. Davis one. As there was not the remotest chance of the election of a Democrat, what the Democratic Electors did with their votes did not really matter in the least.

Another interesting incident occurred in 1912. In that year also the popular election was held on November 5. The Electors were to meet on January 13, 1913. The Vice-President, James S. Sherman, who had been nominated for re-election on the Republican ticket, died on October 30. It so happened that in this instance provision had been made for meeting such a situation. In its closing hours the Republican convention in June had passed a resolution authorizing the national committee to fill any vacancy on the ticket that might be caused by the death or disability of Mr. Taft (who was the party's candidate for re-election to the Presidency) or Mr. Sherman. This was done in such a way that it attracted no attention at the time. It was due to the fact that the managers of the convention were aware that Mr. Sherman's death was expected in the near future.[1] The Republican national committee met hurriedly after Mr. Sherman's death, and decided that, as it was a question not of the Presidency but of the Vice-Presidency, it would not be worth while to complete the ticket until after the popular election. So that year the Republicans throughout the country cast their votes for Electors without knowing who would be Vice-President if their party was successful. The polling on November 5 showed that here, again, the choice of a substitute would be a mere formality. The committee, however, solemnly conferred together on November 12 and decided on a distinguished University President as the person for whom the Republican Electors should vote. With equal solemnity four Republican Electors in Vermont and four in Utah met on the appointed day in their respective State capitals, and cast for this gentleman the eight votes which were all that had been saved, out of a total Electoral vote of 531, from the wreck of orthodox Republicanism.

But what would happen in the event of the death not of an unsuccessful but of a successful candidate during the interval between the popular election and the meeting of the Electoral Colleges? Would the Electors then regain their independence? Dr. Von Holst, as we have already seen, believed that they would. 'If Horace Greeley,' he remarked in

[1] See *American Review of Reviews*, December 1912, p. 644.

the same passage, ' had been not the defeated but the victorious candidate, the Constitution by his death in 1872 would have come to its rights.' No one, of course, can pronounce an authoritative dictum on the subject, but there is reason to believe that Dr. Von Holst was mistaken. To leave the selection of the President to the unfettered discretion of the Electors of the majority party would be to run the risk of making a present of the office to the minority party, which would concentrate its Electoral votes on one man while those of the majority Electors were scattered. Every possible effort would naturally be made to prevent such a dénoument. The solution that seems to find most favour when this problem is discussed is that the national committee of the party should be called together and should take upon itself the responsibility of giving instructions to the Electors. This course, as mentioned above, was provisionally authorized by the Republican convention in 1912, and it would probably be adopted, with or without any such authorization, if the emergency arose. One can conceive the possibility that an Elector here and there might balk.

' I accepted the office of Elector,' this nonconformist might say, ' on the understanding that I should cast my vote for A. I should not have consented to serve if I had expected to be asked to support B., whom I do not wish to see in the White House. B. is not the choice of the rank and file of the party, as expressed through their delegates at the national convention, but is now being foisted on us by a dictatorial oligarchy. I shall therefore exercise my constitutional right of voting for whomsoever I please.'

AN ELEVENTH-HOUR PROBLEM

But party 'regularity' ranks so high among the virtues of the American politician that very few men would dare to flout the authority of the committee in this way. Obviously, however, there would be an opportunity for some mutually profitable political 'deals' between the committee and any Elector who hesitated to fall into line.

But suppose the death of the Presidential candidate of the majority took place at the eleventh hour—on the day, let us say, before the meeting of the Electoral Colleges, when there was no longer a sufficient margin of time to allow for the summoning of a conference of the party leaders. Presumably the capacity of the long-distance telephone would then be tested to the utmost, but even with its assistance the attempt to secure a general agreement on a single candidate might end in a fiasco. It would be extremely difficult to prevent the scattering of the Electoral votes of the majority party among several candidates, in which case the candidate of the minority party might be elected.

It is inconceivable that, in any event, the intentions of the framers of the Fundamental Law would be carried out. If, in consequence of the death of the successful candidate during the November-January interval, the Electors of the majority party took their orders from a national committee instead of from a national convention, they would equally have forfeited their independence. If they acted on their own discretion, and the scattering of their votes led to the election of the candidate of the opposing party, he would go to the White House as the choice of several State groups of Electors who had carried out the instructions of the convention of their party according to usage. If they were able to act independently without letting in their opponent, the new President would have been chosen by Electors who had exercised their unfettered judgment, and so far the purpose of the Fundamental Law would have been fulfilled. But it would not have been fulfilled altogether. For it was intended not only that the election should be freely made by men who were not hampered by any instructions from outside, but that the Electors themselves should have been appointed in the first place as the persons deemed most suitable to discharge this responsibility. And that element in the process would obviously have been lacking. The men nominated for the position of Presidential Elector at the party conventions and appointed at the November pollings are by no means of the type that would be chosen if it were anticipated that the casting of their votes in January would be more than a formality. Their exercise of the power thus unexpectedly committed to them would therefore be a sort of usurpation. It would certainly fail to carry out the original intention that the President should be chosen by Electors who had been appointed on the ground of their freedom from party obligations and their special fitness to weigh judicially the respective qualifications of possible occupants of the supreme office.

The one safe prediction as to the course of events

A SAFE PREDICTION

in such an emergency is, indeed, that whatever happened would never be allowed to happen again. There would speedily be adopted an amendment to the Fundamental Law, which, by some means or other, would effectually prevent the recurrence of such a confused situation.

III
'ACCIDENTAL' PRESIDENTS

It will probably come to most English readers of this book as a surprise—and, I am afraid, to American readers as a shock—when I include among the usages of the American Constitution the succession of a Vice-President to a Presidency left vacant by the death of its occupant. I am not denying that on the death of Mr. Harding, for instance, Mr. Coolidge became President of the United States, but I affirm that he became so by virtue not of a provision of the Fundamental Law of the Constitution but of one of its usages.

That an 'accidental President,' to use a popular term, is really President admits of no doubt. He is so recognized not only in the newspaper press and in the historical text-books but in every official document. Every American boy or girl is taught at school that when a President dies the Vice-President automatically succeeds him. In the lists of past Presidents published in the year-books, 'accidental' Presidents figure equally with those that have been elected, and they are always reckoned in when one is calculating the chronological place that any individual occupies in the series. After August 2, 1923, everyone spoke of President Coolidge and no one

A POPULAR ERROR

of Vice-President Coolidge, and his right to the title was taken for granted not only by officials in the executive branch of the government but by the legislative and judicial branches also. It is commonly believed that he became President in accordance with a provision made by the Fundamental Law of the Constitution for meeting the emergency caused by the death of his predecessor. That this belief is entirely mistaken would be admitted at once by any intelligent adult who came to the study of the Fundamental Law for the first time and interpreted it for himself without any prepossessions derived from acquaintance with the orthodox doctrine. It is usage, and usage alone, that transforms a Vice-President into a President in such a contingency.

Let us turn to the law and the testimony, keeping meanwhile at the back of our minds the phraseology of the same document respecting the election of a Chief Executive. The person, it says, who is found to have the greatest number of electoral votes ' shall be the President.' Now let us read what is said on the question at issue. ' In case of the removal of the President from office, or of his death, resignation, or inability to discharge the powers and duties of the said office '—what then ? Not ' the Vice-President shall be the President ' nor ' the Vice-President shall become the President,' but ' the same,'—*i.e.* the powers and duties of the presidential office—' shall devolve on the Vice-President.' There is nothing here to prevent you, in such a case, from giving the title of Acting President to the Vice-

President if you wish to. If it is desired to distinguish him from a Vice-President who is not called upon to undertake presidential duties, that is indeed the term that exactly fits the situation. He might appropriately sign himself ' President Acting,' just as the Assistant-Secretary of State, if in charge of the department during a vacancy in the Secretaryship, signs himself ' Secretary of State Acting.' But there is no warrant here for speaking of him as President. By using the language which is actually employed, the framers of the Fundamental Law, one might almost say, go out of their way to make it clear that, though discharging presidential duties, he is not to receive the title of President, pure and simple.

But let us resume our study of the text. ' And the Congress,' this passage continues, 'may by law provide for the case of removal, death, resignation, or inability, both of the President and Vice-President, declaring what officer shall then act as President.' The language of the document, it will be noticed, is carefully consistent with that employed just before. Like the Vice-President on whom the duties of the presidential office fall, the officer who comes next is not to ' be President ' or to ' become President,' but to ' act as President.' There follows immediately yet another clear indication of the distinction to be drawn between a President and a person upon whom accidental circumstances impose the responsibilities of Chief Executive. ' And such officer shall act accordingly, until the disability be removed, or a President shall be elected.' Not 'until another President shall be elected' or 'until the next President shall be elected,' but 'until a President shall be elected.' Nothing could indicate more clearly that, when a President dies, the assumption of his duties by another person does not provide the country with a President. There is no President in being, and there can be none until one is created by the method of election.

Another passage that casts light on the subject is to be found in that part of the Twelfth Amendment which prescribes what shall be done in the event of the failure of any candidate to secure the requisite majority of the votes either of the Presidential Electors or of the House of Representatives. 'Then,' we read, 'the Vice-President shall act as President, as in the case of the death or other constitutional disability of the President.' The use of this analogy once more makes it clear that, in the passage first cited, 'the same shall devolve upon the Vice-President' is meant to be equivalent to 'the Vice-President shall act as President.'

Further, let us notice the language used in Article I., section 3, paragraph 5. 'The Senate shall choose their other officers, and also a President, *pro tempore*, in the absence of the Vice-President, or when he shall exercise the office of President of the United States.' It is not 'when he shall have become President'—which would have been the natural thing to say if it had been intended to make a President of him—but 'when he shall exercise the office of President.' In keeping with this distinction is the fact that what the Senate has to do in the circumstances mentioned is to elect merely a President *pro tempore* of the Senate, and not a Vice-President of the United States. There is no vacancy in the Vice-Presidency, and therefore there is no need or possibility of the appointment of another person to the post. Indeed, it is only now that its occupant begins to remind his fellow-citizens that it was to the Vice-Presidency of the United States that he was primarily elected, and not to the Presidency of the Senate. It is now for the first time that he acts *vice* the President. For it is a mistake to suppose that presiding over the Senate is the chief duty of the Vice-President. In fact, it is no duty of the Vice-President's at all. It is the duty of the President of the Senate. The Fundamental Law, it is true, provides that the offices of Vice-President of the United States and President of the Senate shall be held by the same person, but they are not the same office, and the two titles are not convertible terms. The Vice-President, the text runs, ' shall be President of the Senate,' not ' shall preside over the Senate.' Strictly speaking, the person elected to the Vice-Presidency is the holder of a dormant commission, and he does not render the service for which his office was created until an emergency requires him to act as the President's substitute. As, however, such an emergency is likely to be infrequent, the Fundamental Law saves him from the discomfort of feeling himself *de trop* by coupling with his

THE VICE-PRESIDENCY 63

sinecure a post that has actual duties attached to it as long as Congress is in session. In so doing, that document carefully indicates that the two offices are not to be confused, or regarded as a single office. Whenever it has occasion to refer to the duties the holder of them has to perform *qua* President of the Senate, it mentions him by that title and not as Vice-President of the United States. To whom are the certificates of the voting by the Presidential Electors to be transmitted ? Not to the Vice-President of the United States but to the President of the Senate. And so, when the Vice-President is called away to exercise presidential functions, the Senate has to elect not another Vice-President of the United States but a President *pro tempore* of the Senate. The man who was elected Vice-President is still Vice-President, but, as the Vice-Presidency is now no longer a sinecure, some one else must be found to discharge for the time being the duties of President of the Senate.

That is the only possible conclusion as to the conception of the situation in the minds of the framers of the Constitution of 1787. To-day, on the other hand, it is always taken for granted that the assumption of Presidential duties by a Vice-President leaves the Vice-Presidency vacant. On August 3, 1923, for instance, there appeared in the American papers an Associated Press dispatch from Washington headed ' Vice-Presidency Vacant.' The text of the dispatch began : ' With Calvin Coolidge elevated to the Presidency, the nation now finds itself without a Vice-President.' So, too, Mr. Woodrow Wilson, at the end of the chapter on the Senate in his *Congressional Government*, says of the Vice-President :

> ' His official stature is not to be compared with that of the Speaker of the House of Representatives. So long as he is Vice-President, he is inseparable officially from the Senate ; his importance consists in the fact that he may cease to be Vice-President.'

But if there is a vacancy in the Vice-Presidency it is clearly due not to conformity to the Fundamental Law but to the establishment of a constitutional usage independent of it.

That the view here taken of the meaning of the Fundamental Law is the correct one will be confirmed by a consideration of one incidental result of the common misconception. The scheme as it stands is consistent and complete. But the popular interpretation would mar it in one essential particular. The members of the Convention of 1787 were providing, we must remember, not only for the removal of the President from office, or his death or resignation, but also for his inability to discharge his functions. In the event of his removal, death, or resignation, there would be no intrinsic difficulty in the Vice-President's becoming President, for the office would *ipso facto* have become vacant. But a President incapacitated for his duties still remains President, and the promotion of the Vice-President to the Presidency in such a case would result in there being two Presidents at the same time—which is

THE TERM 'ACT'   65

absurd. If, on the other hand, the Vice-President merely becomes Acting President or Deputy President no such absurdity arises.

But the matter is really set beyond doubt by the language of the document itself. The terminology ' shall act as President ' is decisive. When a person ' acts as ' somebody or something, in order to perform functions that would otherwise be left undischarged, he is not himself that somebody or something, whether he be a guardian who acts as parent, or a secretary who acts as treasurer, or a railway clerk who helps to break a strike by acting as a porter, or a purser who acts as ship's chaplain, or a chauffeur who acts as butler.

To sum up then : (1) The Fundamental Law of the Constitution recognizes two and only two ways by which anyone may become President of the United States ; namely, (a) choice by the Electors, and (b) choice by the House of Representatives on the failure of the Electors to give the requisite majority to any candidate. (2) It admits of no ' presidential succession ' except the following of one elected President by another elected President, either immediately or after an interval. (3) It provides that the duties and powers of the President, in the event of a vacancy occurring during a Presidential term, shall devolve upon the Vice-President, and it does so in language so carefully guarded as to preclude his being considered to have thereby become President. (4) It makes similar provision for the carrying on of the government during the inability or disability—the framers of the Constitution use either term indifferently, evidently regarding the two words as synonymous—of the President. It contemplates the possibility that this inability will be only temporary, in which case the President will presently resume his functions and the Vice-President will go back to the performance of the duties of President of the Senate. (5) It makes it clear that the assumption by the Vice-President of the responsibility of discharging the President's duties creates no vacancy in the Vice-Presidency, but results only, as far as that office is concerned, in the appointment of a substitute to preside over the Senate. (6) This conception of the status of a Vice-President called to the White House is consistently maintained in three different sections of the text of the Fundamental Law, widely separated from one another, and there is not a line in the document that gives even the faintest shadow of support to any other theory.

There is nothing at all peculiar or unusual in this scheme for temporarily supplying the place of the head of a government in an emergency. In monarchical countries—Great Britain, for example—a regency is a close parallel. A regent exercises all the functions of royalty. He lives in a palace, and maintains the dignity of a regal court; he receives ambassadors from foreign Powers; he summons and dissolves parliaments; he appoints high officers of state; he signs royal warrants and proclamations; in short, he does all that may become a king. But he is not a king, and he does not figure in the roll of kings as one of the succession. When George III. became unable to bear the responsibilities of the Crown his eldest son was appointed to undertake them with the style of regent. The term of George IV.'s reign, however, is counted from 1820, when he succeeded to the throne on his father's death, and not from 1811, when he became regent. Another interesting analogy is supplied by the present-day administration of self-governing colonies within the British Empire. Each of the States of the Australian Commonwealth has not only a Governor but a Lieutenant-Governor, who is usually the Chief Justice of the Supreme Court. As long as the Governor is in residence and capable of exercising his functions the duties of the Lieutenant-Governor are nil. But should the Governor leave the State for even a few days, or should he become so ill as to be incapable of discharging his duties, the Lieutenant-Governor takes his place. The Lieutenant-Governor also administers the government in the interval, if such there occur, between the departure of one Governor and the arrival of his successor. Now a Lieutenant-Governor whose dormant commission has thus become operative possesses every whit as much authority as a Governor. He receives, moreover, equal honours, even to the playing of the national anthem when he enters the Governor's box at the theatre. But during this period of office he is always styled not Governor but Acting Governor. When he dies the obituary notices in the press will say of him that he administered the government so many times or that he was Acting Governor so many times, but will never speak of him as having been Governor. One might also compare the status of an Acting President to that of a chargé d'affaires at an embassy or legation, who keeps its business going during the absence of the ambassador or minister.

There is no need, however, to go so far afield for parallels. They may be found, within America itself, in almost every business or institution. When the editor of a newspaper goes off on a holiday the ' powers and duties ' of his office may ' devolve ' on some member of his staff, but this temporary devolution is not equivalent to the appointment of that substitute as editor. Similarly, when a college president is away from the campus or ill, some member of the faculty takes over the reins, but that does not mean that he has become president of the college.

How, then, has it come about that usage has thus magnified the status of an Acting President? It has been said that Great Britain acquired her colonial empire in a fit of absence of mind, and very much the same explanation may be given of the development we are now considering. The change was not deliberately made. There was never a moment when the American people said : ' Go to, now, let us make the Acting President a President.' The transformation was effected, almost by inadvertence, and certainly without any realization of what was involved in it, on the first occasion when a President

JOHN TYLER

died during his term of office, *i.e.* on the death of President W. H. Harrison a few weeks after his inauguration in 1841.

The story is thus told by Col. A. K. McClure in his well-known history of the Presidency:

> 'John Tyler,' he says, 'was Vice-President, and was living quietly on his farm on the Virginia Peninsula. He could not be reached by railways, and telegraphs were unknown. He had no knowledge that he had become President through the death of Harrison until late the next day, when Webster and another member of the Cabinet finally found their way to his home, partly by water and partly overland, and formally announced to him the death of the President and the new duties which devolved upon him. He hastened to Washingtom to find a very grave dispute among the leading statesmen of both parties as to whether he became President or simply Acting President. It was important to determine whether he was President with the full title. The question was brought up in Congress, and in the midst of a discussion on the subject a message was received from the Executive Mansion signed "John Tyler, President." The dispute was at once ended, and the question settled for all time.'[1]

It is a pity to have to spoil so entertaining a story of how the confident 'gesture,' as we should call it nowadays, of an ambitious politician who knew his own mind, when other authorities were in a strait betwixt two opinions, added in perpetuity a new usage to the American Constitution. But a scrutiny of contemporary records compels a revision of Col.

[1] Col. A. K. McClure, *Our Presidents and how we make them*, ed. 1902, p. 74.

McClure's version in certain important particulars. President Harrison died on April 4, in the early hours of the morning. His Cabinet, meeting before the end of the same day, issued a public announcement of his death and at the same time sent a notice of it to Tyler, whom they addressed as 'Vice-President of the United States.' This communication, however, was entirely silent as to any responsibilities thereby cast upon its recipient. On April 6, in the presence of the Cabinet, the oath of office was taken by Tyler in the following terms :

> 'I do solemnly swear that I will faithfully execute the office of President of the United States, and will to the best of my ability preserve, protect, and defend the Constitution of the United States.'

The certificate of the judge who administered the oath runs thus :

> 'I, William Cranch, chief judge of the circuit court of the District of Columbia, certify that the above-named John Tyler personally appeared before me this day, and although he deems himself qualified to perform the duties and exercise the powers and offices of President on the death of William Henry Harrison, late President of the United States, without any other oath than that which he has taken as Vice-President, yet as doubts may arise, and for greater caution, took and subscribed the foregoing oath before me.'

This conviction of Tyler's that the oath he had taken as Vice-President did not really require to be supplemented is one of the most singular features of the whole affair. For it gives away his entire case. If he had become no more than Acting President,

TYLER'S SECOND OATH

the oath he had previously taken to discharge faithfully the duties of the Vice-Presidency would cover the whole ground, as one of the prescribed duties of that office—indeed, its only duty, if, as I hold, the Vice-Presidency of the United States is distinct from the Presidency of the Senate—is that of acting as President in the event of the President's death. But if, on the other hand, as he contended throughout, his Vice-Presidency had now come to an end and he had become possessed of the Presidency as fully as any person elected to that office, then his assumption of his new dignity must needs require him to take the oath incumbent upon all new Presidents.

Tyler's first public proclamation from the White House was issued on April 9 and was addressed to 'the people of the United States.' He spoke of himself as having been called ' to the high office of President of this Confederacy,' and made a statement of the principles that would govern him in the general course of his administration of public affairs, as ' the usual opportunity which is afforded to a Chief Magistrate ' of delivering an inaugural address had, under the peculiar circumstances, not been afforded to him. At the time of Harrison's death Congress was not in session, but, by a proclamation issued by the late President on March 17, it had been summoned to meet on May 31. Immediately it convened there was proposed in the House a resolution in the usual form, appointing a committee to wait on the President and inform him that Congress was ready to proceed to business. An amendment was offered to strike out the word 'President' and insert instead the words 'Vice-President, now exercising the office of President.' In the Senate, on June 1, it was proposed to amend a similar motion by substituting for 'President' the words 'Vice-President, on whom, by the death of the late President, the powers and duties of the office of President have devolved.' The amendments were defeated, in the Senate by thirty-eight to eight and in the House by a vote which is not recorded.

In those days, unfortunately, there was as yet no *Congressional Record*, and the summaries of the debates in the *Congressional Globe* are too brief to give us much enlightenment. In the House, Tyler's principal spokesman, Representative H. A. Wise, of Virginia, declared himself to know, as a fact, that 'the present incumbent would claim the position that he was, by the Constitution, by election, and by the act of God, President of the United States.' Ordinarily a new President is content if he can lay claim to the first two of these titles to his office. (The second, of course, if it has any meaning, is really included in the first, but logic was evidently not a strong point with John Tyler.) When Tyler arrogated to himself, in addition, a Divine sanction which had not been accorded to any of his predecessors, not even to George Washington, the cumulative effect of this exceptional authority seems to have overawed the House. In the Senate debate the most notable argument was that of Senator Walker, of Mississippi, that 'the same,' in the text of the

Fundamental Law, meant not 'the powers and duties' of the Presidential office but 'the office' itself, and this, in his opinion, was a vital and decisive difference. No sooner had this debate closed and the vote been taken than Tyler's first message to Congress was received and read. In the first paragraph he spoke of his 'accession to the Presidency,' but incidentally he threw over, by anticipation, the chief contention that had just been made in his favour. 'By the provisions of the Fundamental Law,' he said, 'the powers and duties of the high station to which he [Harrison] was elected have devolved upon me.'

The question was never again raised in Congress, and Tyler's usurpation was sanctioned by the acquiescence of the country. There might remain some individual objectors who were of their own opinion still, but in the end they yielded to the majority. In the memoirs, for instance, of ex-President John Quincy Adams we find him recording on April 4, 1841, that the death of Harrison makes John Tyler 'Acting President of the Union for four years less one month.' On April 7 he mentions 'the Acting President' as taking part in Harrison's funeral. On April 16 there is this entry :

> 'I paid a visit this morning to Mr. Tyler, who styles himself President of the United States and not Vice-President acting as President, which would be the correct style. But it is a construction in direct violation both of the grammar and context of the Constitution, which confers upon the Vice-President, on the decease of the

President, not the office but the powers and duties of the said office.'

In later entries he refers to Tyler, for a short period, as Acting President, but later he comes to speak of him always as President. A letter of Tyler's written three years after the end of his term shows that by that time the few remaining dissentients had been reduced to a policy of pin-pricks. In 1848, writing to Buchanan, then Secretary of State, to acknowledge the receipt of a package, he says:

' I cannot recognize myself in the address of *ex-vice-president*; for the *third* time, it is repeated in annual communications from your department, and obviously arises from a studied purpose. I feel convinced that it has been without your sanction or direction, but proceeds, in what spirit I will not undertake to say, from some subaltern in your department. I desire only to say that if I am addressed, and especially from the State Department, by a title, it must be by that which the Constitution confers, which has been recognized by the country and all departments of its government, and has been used in the public correspondence with foreign nations, in the ratification of treaties, and approval of the laws.'

A few days later Tyler informed his son that the last mail had brought him an entirely ' apologetic ' letter from Buchanan.[1]

Five times since then has a Vice-President been called to the White House through the death of its occupant—Fillmore through Taylor's death in 1850, Johnson through Lincoln's in 1865, Arthur through Garfield's in 1881, Roosevelt through M'Kinley's

[1] Lyon G. Tyler, *Letters and Times of the Tylers,* vol. ii. p. 13.

ANDREW JOHNSON

in 1910, and Coolidge through Harding's in 1923. In only one instance does there seem to have been the slightest hesitation, either popular or official, in according to the Acting President the full status and title of President.

That exception occurred in connection with the impeachment of Andrew Johnson. We learn from the most authoritative account of the proceedings against him [1] that the first movement to depose him was made when Representative Ashley rose in the House to impeach ' Andrew Johnson, Vice-President and Acting President of the United States ' of high crimes and misdemeanours, and to submit a resolution authorizing the committee on the judiciary ' to inquire into the official conduct of Andrew Johnson, Vice-President of the United States, discharging the powers and duties of the office of President of the United States.' The resolution was adopted, but somehow the terms of the proposed indictment altered their shape in passing through the mill of the judiciary committee. The report presented by that committee, when its deliberations were completed, concerned the impeachment of ' the President of the United States,' and the same terms were used in the subsequent resolutions of the House, in the House's notification to the Senate, and in the actual trial. We find, however, that at one stage of the proceedings the question of the correctness of this terminology was definitely raised.

[1] D. M. Dewitt, *The Impeachment and Trial of Andrew Johnson*, ed. 1903, p. 152.

'From the time of Johnson's accession,' says Mr. Dewitt, 'the more spiteful of his adversaries were addicted to the habit of denying he was President, asserting that he was still Vice-President and for the time being only "Acting President." And yet by the articles reported he was impeached as "President of the United States." Mr. Boutwell affected apprehension that the Senate might decide that Johnson was not President, and in that case the whole proceedings would have to be gone over from the beginning. "A different court," he said, "must be organized for the trial of the Vice-President from that authorized by the Constitution to try the President."[1]

It turned out, however, that Representative Boutwell need not have been uneasy, for the Senate made no difficulty about regarding Johnson as President, and it was accordingly the impeachment not of a Vice-President but of a President that was thereupon tried in that body.

The usage, then, which has made a full President of what was meant to be an Acting President is as firmly established to-day as any constitutional practice outside the Fundamental Law can possibly be.

'But,' some one may object, 'what does the difference amount to, after all? Is there anything involved beyond a rather pedantic question of terminological exactitude? It is agreed that there devolve upon the Vice-President in such an emergency all the functions of the Presidency, so that, whatever the Fundamental Law declares that a President shall do or may do, this substitute or successor, by whichever name you like to call him, must do or

[1] *Op. cit.* p. 380.

THE ROLL OF PRESIDENTS 77

may do. Seeing, then, that his powers and responsibilities remain exactly the same in either case, does it matter in the least whether you call him President or Acting President ? '

It matters, I suggest, a great deal. It has already mattered so much that it has profoundly influenced not only national but international affairs.

Before we consider the graver consequences involved, it is worth while to note the minor point that the establishment of this usage has completely obliterated, in the lists of past Presidents of the United States, the distinction between those persons who have administered the affairs of the nation in virtue of having been elected President and those upon whom the task has fallen through another cause than their being regarded, by a majority of the electors, as the fittest men to be entrusted with it. However well America's ' accidental ' Presidents may have acquitted themselves and to whatever degree they may have deserved the gratitude of their fellow-citizens for their services, it does not appear quite seemly that their names should appear on the roll of Chief Executives as of equal rank with those whom the nation called to the Presidency by its deliberate choice.

But the establishment of the usage has done a great deal more than this. It has practically nullified the provision made by the Fundamental Law for the administration of the government when a President who has not died or resigned or been removed from office by impeachment has become for any reason temporarily incapacitated for the performance of his duties. His 'inability' might be the result of any one of a variety of causes. He might be seriously ill, or he might be absent from the country, or, in time of war, he might be captured by the enemy. (In 1814, when the national capital was occupied by a British force, President Madison had to seek safety in flight, and during the Civil War President Lincoln once narrowly escaped capture.) Attention has often been called to a serious gap in the American political system owing to the lack of any prescribed method of determining whether or not a President is incapacitated by illness. There can be no controversy about a death or resignation or removal, but who is to decide whether a President has become unfit to discharge his duties? It would certainly not be safe to leave the decision to the man himself, especially if his illness took the form of some mental disorder. The Fundamental Law itself is silent on this point, and the gap has not been filled by any statute. In 1881 this question came into prominence through the illness of President Garfield, who was shot on July 2 and lingered on until September 19. In his first annual message to Congress on December 6 President Arthur emphasized the necessity of settling the disputed questions involved in such a situation and submitted them to the 'early and thoughtful consideration' of that body. Nothing, however, has been done from that day until now to clear up the uncertainties lurking in the word 'inability.' (It is worth noting, by the way, that according to the Provisional Constitution of the Confederate States the ' inability ' of a Confederate President was to be determined by a vote of two-thirds of the Confederate Congress. This provision, however, was not repeated in the permanent Constitution.)

Perhaps the indifference of Congress to President Arthur's exhortation and to subsequent appeals is due to a sub-conscious feeling that the question who shall decide on a President's ' inability ' is really an academic one. It has been made so by the usage which has transformed a Vice-President performing presidential functions into a full President. For the provision of the Fundamental Law for the carrying on of the government during a President's ' inability ' has thereby been made a dead letter. If a Vice-President still remains Vice-President while acting as President, there is still only one President of the United States—the man, chosen at the last election, who, though temporarily unable to perform his duties, cannot cease to be President except by death, resignation, or removal. But, as pointed out earlier in this chapter, if you make the Vice-President a President you are confronted in such circumstances with the absurd and impossible situation of having two Presidents at the same moment. This absurdity is quite independent of the difficulty of deciding whether the elected President is incapacitated or not, and it would not be relieved in any degree by the enactment of a statute prescribing the way in which the doubt as to the elected President's condition should be settled.

So the knot is cut by refraining altogether from utilizing the services of the Vice-President to perform presidential functions when the President himself is unequal to them. And the net result is to leave the government without an actual Chief Executive whenever the elected President is no longer physically or mentally competent to discharge his duties. The Fundamental Law met this emergency by providing that the Vice-President should in such a case act as President. Usage, however, has transformed the intended substitute into a successor, and for a successor there can be no room until the elected President either dies or becomes a private citizen.

To find an example of the practical nullifying of the Fundamental Law through this usage we need go no further back than the long and serious illness of President Woodrow Wilson. One of the chapters of Mr. David Lawrence's *True Story of Woodrow Wilson* is appropriately headed, ' When America had no active President.' For several months the executive side of the government of the United States lay in a kind of twilight zone. The American public did not know then, and does not know to-day, by whom and in what manner the duties of Chief Executive were discharged during that period. The one certain thing is that they were not discharged by the person and in the manner prescribed by the Fundamental Law. Some of them were simply not discharged at all. One of the duties of the President is to ' receive ambassadors and other public ministers,' but Viscount Grey spent four months at

WOODROW WILSON

Washington as British Ambassador without once seeing the head of the State.

During the period of the President's illness there came up for settlement the question of the part America should take in the political reconstruction of a world shattered by the Great War. Everything hung upon the possibility of co-operation between the President and the Senate. But while the Senate was debating the Versailles Treaty the President was on his sick-bed and unable to profit by the advice of his normal counsellors. In March, 1920, it was finally demonstrated that the treaty would be unacceptable to the Senate unless modified by the Lodge reservations. In the third week of April the President met his Cabinet for the first time for eight months. Meanwhile the guardians of his bedside had exercised a rigid censorship of their own over the admission of visitors to his room, opening the door to one man and closing it to another as they themselves saw fit.

> 'Those who had it in their power,' says Mr. David Lawrence, ' to persuade President Wilson to permit advisers to reach him failed to realise the immensity of their responsibility in shutting him off so completely from the outside world. Whether America would have benefited by entrance into the League of Nations it is not necessary to discuss, but the United States would to-day be in the League officially if the President had been able to get the advice he so much needed in his enfeebled condition. On his sick-bed he almost agreed to accept the Lodge reservations, but some one urged him to make

of it an issue in the 1920 campaign, and in January, 1920, he asked that a solemn referendum be taken.'[1]

Elsewhere in the same book Mr. Lawrence declares that

'had he retained his health, Woodrow Wilson, just as sure as day follows night, would have accepted the Lodge reservations to the Versailles Treaty and secured thereby for the United States a membership in the League of Nations. He was almost persuaded to do so on his sick-bed, but his illness induced a consciousness of incertitude which together with the exclusion of outside advice made him irritable and inflexible.'[2]

Thus the falling into desuetude, through usage, of the provision of the Fundamental Law expressly designed to provide for such an emergency, left the deciding voice in this crisis to an invalid instead of to a hale man.

The usage discussed in this chapter affected the course of international events at an even earlier stage. For it had made the Fundamental Law a dead letter in the situation occasioned by another type of 'inability.' President Wilson's visit to Europe at the end of 1918 was clearly one of the emergencies provided for in the clause relating to the assumption of the duties of the Presidency by the Vice-President. It has often been remarked, with reference to the old tradition that the President should not leave the territory of the United States during his term, that there is nothing in the Fundamental Law to prohibit him from going abroad. There was no need for

[1] D. Lawrence, *The True Story of Woodrow Wilson*, ed. 1924, p. 299.
[2] *Op. cit.* p. 16.

any such restriction. His absence could be regarded with perfect equanimity, no matter how far he went or how long he stayed away, for the device of a Vice-Presidential substitute had ensured the efficient carrying on of the government meanwhile.

No unprejudiced person can doubt that a President who is separated from the seat of government by three thousand miles, especially while Congress is in session, is incapacitated by physical distance from the performance of the duties of his office. Think, for a moment, of what those duties include. He is to give Congress from time to time information of the state of the Union and recommend legislative measures to their consideration. He is to exercise his judgment upon every bill that has been passed by both Houses. The maximum period allowed him for such consideration is ten days, the intention of the Fundamental Law being that objectors to a bill may during this time lay their case before him. If he does not return it to Congress within ten days the bill becomes law, just as if he had signed it. In the event of disagreement between the two Houses as to the time of adjournment he is to decide between them. He is responsible for the appointment of innumerable public officials. The granting of reprieves and pardons for offences against the United States—a matter which conceivably may need prompt action—is his, and his alone. And beyond all this he is to ' take care that the laws be faithfully executed.' In fulfilment of this latter charge he may even be confronted with the responsibility of granting or refusing an application from the authorities of a State to send United States troops into it for its protection against domestic violence. I invite anyone to meditate upon the sections of the Fundamental Law which set forth the powers and duties of the Chief Executive and then say whether, with all the assistance that mail and telegraph can give, these powers can be properly exercised and these duties adequately discharged by an absentee President—by a President, for example, who for several months is ' ez fur away ez Payris is.'[1] Remember, too, that in this instance the absentee President was not a man on a holiday, with several hours a day free to devote to any problems that might be communicated to him by the subordinates he had left behind. His attention was being continuously absorbed by a task which demanded all his energies. A distinguished American financier who was in Paris at the time describes the President as studying papers and documents until late at night, and says of him that ' he was, by all odds, the hardest worked man at the Conference.'[2]

It is simply childish to suggest that, in such circumstances, anyone who lacked the power of working miracles could concurrently discharge the responsibilities of the Presidency of the United States. Even for a President who attempts to

[1] Except for a brief visit home between February 24 and March 5, 1919, President Wilson was continuously absent from the United States from December 4, 1918, to July 8, 1919.

[2] T. W. Lamont, quoted by Charles Seymour, *Woodrow Wilson and the World War*, ed. 1921, p. 12, footnote.

discharge them in Washington, with no other task to divide his attention, these responsibilities are normally almost overwhelming. No one can read the descriptions of the everyday routine of the White House which appear from time to time in the press under such headings as ' A President's Day ' without being convinced that his task is one for a superman. The death of Mr. Wilson's immediate successor was commonly attributed to the excessive labours of his office, and it occasioned numerous speeches and newspaper articles urging that some means should be found of lightening burdens too heavy for any one man to bear. ' One urgent reform demanded,' said Representative T. E. Burton in his ' keynote speech ' at the Republican National Convention of 1924, ' is that the President be relieved of part of his most exacting duties. A constitution of iron can hardly bear up under the strain imposed upon the Chief Magistrate.' A member of his own Cabinet has thus spoken of the demands made upon the strength of President Wilson himself at the White House under normal conditions :

> ' There is sound reason for the President's personal physician being near at hand, for the task is such that daily watchfulness must be used to keep his physical and mental powers at highest pitch.... If the country once visualized the hard labor the President has daily to perform, a change would be made.' [1]

Is it conceivable that the demands of such an office could be adequately met three thousand miles away

[1] W. C. Redfield, *With Congress and Cabinet*, ed. 1924, p. 94.

in the odds and ends of time left over from the exhausting duties of the Peace Conference?

Here, surely, was an occasion, if ever there was one, for bringing into operation the expedient provided by the Fundamental Law for the discharge of presidential functions during the ' inability ' of the President himself. This is not the place to discuss whether or not Mr. Wilson judged rightly that it was desirable for him to be personally present at Paris as the principal representative of the United States Government. My point is that, when he had once taken that decision, an observance of both the letter and the spirit of the Fundamental Law would have required him to hand over the reins of the presidential office for the time to the Vice-President.

But, long before the emergency arose, the establishment of the usage now under discussion had banished altogether from the public mind any thought of having recourse temporarily to the services of the Vice-President in such a case of ' inability.' No one, I suppose, doubts that Mr. Wilson would never have conceived the idea of going abroad if he had believed—and if the American people had believed—that it would involve his ceasing for the time, *ipso facto*, to be the head of the nation, and his handing over the administration of the government to Mr. Marshall during the period of his absence. The clear intent of the Fundamental Law, however, had been obscured long before by the usage which has changed a Vice-President undertaking the duties of Chief Executive from a mere Acting President

FAR-REACHING RESULTS 87

who may perform these duties for a few weeks and months and then go back to the chair of the Senate, into a full President, whose status is equal in all respects of that of the man whose place he takes. But for the establishment of this usage it would have seemed to everyone as much a matter of course that Mr. Marshall should fill the gap when Mr. Wilson went to Europe as that Mr. Coolidge should take over the President's duties on Mr. Harding's death. In that event the whole attitude both of the officials at Washington and of the American people toward Mr. Wilson's going to Europe would have been different; the visit would never have taken place, and what happened at Versailles—and afterward at the Capitol—would have happened otherwise. So the history not only of the United States but of the civilized world has been profoundly affected by a constitutional usage originating, three-quarters of a century ago, in the self-assertion of one of the most bizarre figures that ever appeared on the stage of American politics—a preposterous country lawyer who, after a brief and turbulent period in a high office for which he was conspicuously unfit, subsided into obscurity, and died twenty years later a member of the legislature of a Confederacy then in active rebellion against the nation of which he had once ' accidentally ' become Chief Magistrate.

IV

THIRD PRESIDENTIAL TERMS

THE question of the re-eligibility of a President of the United States was considered by the Convention of 1787, which ultimately decided not to insert in the Fundamental Law any provision that would prevent his election for a second term. The first President was re-elected and several of his successors have enjoyed the same distinction. In every such instance but one the second term immediately followed the first, the exception being Cleveland's second election in 1892 after an interval of four years. The question of a third term did not come up in the Convention at all, and the Fundamental Law is accordingly silent on the subject. Many authorities, however, are of the opinion that usage—or ' the unwritten Constitution,' as they generally call it—forbids a third term. ' It may now be said to be part of the unwritten Constitution,' declares Professor J. A. Woodburn, ' that no President is eligible to a third term.'[1] According to Professor A. B. Hart, ' the country is now absolutely set against third presidential terms under any circumstances.'[2] And Gamaliel Bradford refers to ' the popular prejudice, which has almost

[1] J. A. Woodburn, *The American Republic and its Government*, ed. 1916, p. 115.

[2] A. B. Hart, *Actual Government*, ed. 1918, p. 266.

A CONFLICT OF OPINION

reached the point of superstition, against a third term for any President.'[1] On the other hand, Professor J. B. Thayer demurs to Professor Dicey's positive assertion that it is a convention of the American Constitution that a President shall not be re-elected more than once. 'That is quite over-stated,' he comments. 'We have re-elected our Governors many times, and when we get a good enough President it is possible that no talk of a "third term" will be any serious obstacle to re-electing him repeatedly.'[2] And Lord Bryce, in his last expression of opinion on the question, remarks that 'the American tradition which forbade a person to be chosen President more than twice seems to have recently lost nearly all its influence.'[3]

In view of this conflict of opinion it may be well to record briefly what has happened when the question of a third term has been actually raised. On the completion, in 1792, of his first term in the Presidency George Washington wished to be excused from serving a second. In a letter to Madison he urged that the spirit of American government rendered 'a rotation in its elective officers more congenial with the ideas the people have of liberty and safety.' He was pressed, however, on all sides not to compel the country at that critical stage in its history to make a choice from among the rival statesmen who surrounded him, and he yielded to the general demand.

[1] G. Bradford, *The Lesson of Popular Government*, ed. 1899, vol. i. p. 560, footnote.
[2] J. B. Thayer, *Legal Essays*, ed. 1908, p. 204.
[3] Lord Bryce, *Modern Democracies*, ed. 1921, vol ii. p. 469, footnote.

In 1796 he positively refused to take office a third time. In the introduction of his farewell address to the people of the United States he made no allusion to the principle of rotation in office, but based his refusal on personal reasons only. His acceptance of and continuance in the Presidency had been, he said, a uniform sacrifice of inclination to the opinion of duty and to a deference to what appeared to be the desire of the American people. He had constantly hoped that it would have been much earlier in his power, consistently with motives which he was not at liberty to disregard, to return to that retirement from which he had been reluctantly drawn. At the end of his first term he had abandoned the idea in consequence of mature reflection on the then perplexed and critical posture of American affairs with foreign nations and the unanimous advice of persons entitled to his confidence.

> ' I rejoice,' he concluded, ' that the state of your concerns, external as well as internal, no longer renders the pursuit of inclination incompatible with the sentiment of duty or propriety ; and am persuaded, whatever partiality may be retained for my services, that, in the present circumstances of our country, you will not disapprove my determination to retire.'

In a later paragraph he referred to ' the increasing weight of years '—he was then sixty-four, or just a year younger than Gladstone when he made his premature decision to retire from the Liberal leadership—as admonishing him more and more every day that the shade of retirement was as necessary to him

GENERAL GRANT

as it would be welcome. In 1808, Jefferson was strongly urged to become a candidate for the third time, and it is generally believed that, if he had consented, he would have been elected, but he declined nomination. In 1836 Jackson's great popularity led to a demand for his election for a third term, but he, too, refused. Jackson was himself strongly in favour of amending the Fundamental Law so as to limit the service of the President to a single term of four or six years. He included a recommendation to that effect in his first message to Congress, and repeated it in no less than five of his subsequent annual messages.

From Jackson's time the question disappeared from practical politics until General Grant was approaching the completion of his second term. A proposal to re-elect him aroused keen discussion.[1] The House of Representatives went so far as to pass, in 1876, a resolution stigmatizing this proposal as ' unwise, unpatriotic, and fraught with peril to our free institutions.' The strength of the opposition prevented any attempt being made to nominate Grant at the Republican convention of that year. In 1880, however, after the interval of President Hayes' administration, when Grant's prestige had been enhanced by the almost royal reception given him on his visit to Europe, an earnest effort was

[1] See especially an elaborate article on the subject, occupying eight columns, mostly in small print, in the *New York Tribune* of September 14, 1874. It appeared anonymously, but it was written by John Bigelow, as we learn from his autobiography. This article reviewed in detail the whole history of the subject to that date.

made by some of his friends to secure his nomination. They anticipated that there would be much less popular objection to a third term, separated from the second by an interval of four years, than to three continuous terms. How strongly this movement was supported is shown by the fact that Grant's name led the voting at the convention until the thirty-sixth ' ballot.'

> ' Grant would have been nominated by acclamation,' declares Senator Foraker, ' if it had not been that there was a deep-rooted prejudice in the minds of many of his warmest friends, as well as in the minds of the people generally, against a third term. Washington was still remembered, honoured, and revered by his countrymen. The example he had set had become an unwritten law, and the people were not willing to violate it even for their greatest hero and most popular fellow-countryman.'[1]

It appears that admiration for Grant was not the only motive that brought him votes in the convention. In his account of the incident Senator Foraker tells us that Conkling and Blaine had become bitter enemies ; that Conkling cast about to see how he could head off and defeat Blaine's nomination ; and that it was to accomplish this purpose that he attempted to exploit the popularity of Grant and brought him forward as a candidate.

President Cleveland held office from 1885 to 1889 and again from 1893 to 1897. The convention of his own party in 1896, so far from being inclined to

[1] J. B. Foraker, *Notes of a Busy Life*, ed. 1916, vol. i. p. 140.

CLEVELAND AND ROOSEVELT

nominate him again, included in its platform the following plank:

> 'We declare it to be the unwritten law of this republic, established by custom and usage of a hundred years, and sanctioned by the examples of the greatest and wisest of those who founded and have maintained our government, that no man shall be eligible for a third term of the presidential office.'

On this occasion, comments Mr. Gamaliel Bradford, writing not long after the event, 'the bugbear of a third term was used to defeat the nomination of probably the best and certainly the most available candidate whom the Democratic party had to offer.'[1]

We next come to Theodore Roosevelt, who succeeded to the Presidency on the death of M'Kinley on September 14, 1901. His first tenure of the office therefore lacked the complete term of four years by a period of a few days over six months. Immediately after the election of November, 1904, had shown that he was to remain at the White House, he issued a brief statement, in which he said: 'The wise custom which limits the President to two terms regards the substance and not the form, and under no circumstances will I be a candidate for or accept another nomination.' (This reference to 'the substance and not the form' was, of course, intended to settle the question whether the period of September, 1901—March, 1905, was to be regarded as a first term.) He supplemented this by a further

[1] G. Bradford, *The Lesson of Popular Government*, ed. 1899, vol. i. p. 360, footnote.

statement, sent to an Omaha paper in May, 1905, which ran as follows: ' You are authorized to state that I will not again be a candidate for the office of President of the United States. There are no strings to this statement. I mean it.' In December, 1907, he referred to this announcement and added: ' I have not changed and shall not change the decision thus announced.'[1] The demand for his nomination for a third term persisted for some time in spite of these repeated refusals, but in the end Mr. Roosevelt imposed his own will upon his supporters and induced them to nominate Mr. Taft in his place at the Republican convention of 1908. This result was achieved with great difficulty, and a few votes were actually cast for Mr. Roosevelt at the convention. The ex-President's disappointment with the administration of his successor led to his publishing at the end of January, 1912, a gloss upon the statement he had issued on election night in 1904. The declaration he had then made that he would not accept another nomination really meant that he would not accept such a nomination while holding the office of President. ' It had no application whatever,' he explained, ' to the candidacy of a man who was not at the time in office, whether he had or had not been President before.'[2] In February, 1912, there came to him a request from seven Republican State Governors that he accept the

---

[1] See E. Stanwood, *History of the Presidency from 1897 to 1916*, ed. 1916, pp. 140 and 155.

[2] E. Stanwood, *op. cit.* p. 235.

THE PROGRESSIVE NOMINATION 95

nomination. He replied : ' I will accept the nomination if it is tendered to me, and I will adhere to this decision until the convention has expressed its preference.' The convention expressed its preference by nominating President Taft for re-election on the first ' ballot ' by 561 votes as against 107 cast for Mr. Roosevelt. There followed a split in the Republican party and the summoning, a few weeks later, of a ' Progressive ' convention which gave Mr. Roosevelt an immediate and unanimous nomination. During the election campaign his opponents did their best to utilize against him the alleged popular objection to a third term, while his friends attempted to blunt the argument by pointing out that his candidature was only for a second ' elective ' term. A sensational incident of the campaign is an evidence of the prominence given to this issue in the election controversies. While on one of his speech-making tours, Mr. Roosevelt was shot at by a man of unbalanced mind, who said : ' I shot Theodore Roosevelt because he was a menace to the country. He should not have a third term. I shot him as a warning that men must not try to have more than two terms as President.'

The question might have been put to the test in the career of President Wilson if he had completed his second term in unimpaired physical and mental vigour. According to Mr. David Lawrence he was desirous of a third term in order that he might make a fight for the League of Nations, and he would have sought the nomination in 1920 if he had regained his health.[1] Evidently, then, so high an authority on the American political system as President Wilson did not think the anti-third-term usage so firmly established as to debar all possibility of his own election for a third term.

This review of the history of the subject does not encourage dogmatism, but there are a few points on which one may speak with confidence. In the first place, as a matter of fact, no one has ever held the office of President of the United States for three terms. But this is not in itself decisive as to the existence of a constitutional usage prohibiting a third election. It is equally a fact that no Roman Catholic has ever been elected to the Presidency, but no one would affirm that there is a constitutional usage which closes the door of the White House in the face of Roman Catholics. The most that can be said is that there exists—or is believed to exist—so strong a sentiment against the election of anyone but a Protestant that any Roman Catholic who seeks a presidential nomination is seriously handicapped by his faith. Similarly it is a fact that no Jews or men of colour or corporation lawyers have been elected to the Presidency, but we may not therefore conclude that usage has definitely added any racial or occupational disqualifications to the limitations imposed by the Fundamental Law.

The next undoubted fact to record is that there has been only a single instance in which anyone has

[1] D. Lawrence, *The True Story of Woodrow Wilson*, ed. 1924, pp. 293, 299, 320.

THE FEAR OF A TYRANT 97

received a nomination for a third term. In this case, Mr. Roosevelt's, the nomination was not for a third continuous term, neither was it for a third election, as during the term commonly reckoned as his first he was an 'accidental President.' If his defeat in 1912 may be interpreted as an evidence of the strength of the popular objection to a third term of any kind, it may also be taken to indicate that it is not as widely spread or as deeply rooted as often supposed, for he received more than 4,000,000 votes, running ahead of the orthodox Republican candidate by 642,000.

We should be safe, I think, in concluding that the objection to a third term separated from the second by an interval of four years is less pronounced than to three continuous terms. For in such a case there can be less ground for the apprehension lest a successful candidate, if he were ambitious and unscrupulous, might be tempted to utilize his control of the whole executive branch of the government, not to say his authority as commander-in-chief of the forces, to secure for himself a life tenure. In the chapter on 'Presidential Government' in the first series of his *Historical Essays* Mr. E. A. Freeman recalled that in the early days of the American Republic 'men professed the old Greek fear lest a President often re-elected should grow into a tyrant,' and remarked that experience had shown this fear to be 'quite groundless.' Whether groundless or not, it has not entirely disappeared. The terrifying spectre of a perpetual autocrat in the

White House has seriously disturbed the minds of many Americans in modern times. Even such a man as George Bancroft, when the re-election of Grant was mooted in 1874, could write that 'the nomination of the present incumbent of the Presidency to a third term would in my judgment be a long stride toward changing our republic into a monarchy.'[1] And some of the articles on the subject reprinted in *The Editorials of Henry Watterson* show what a genuine alarm could be felt by one of the most distinguished and influential of American journalists lest Mr. Roosevelt's popularity should tempt him to essay the rôle of a Diaz.

There remains, however, the objection that to give any President a third term, whether consecutive or not, would be to bestow on him a greater honour than was ever conferred on George Washington. At the back of their minds the American people have always the recollection that Washington was only twice elected President. As a mere precedent this fact probably counts for little. Other traditions have been broken, and this might be broken too. What does influence the attitude of Americans is the idea that to grant such a distinction to any living man would imply a disparagement of the greatness of the Father of his Country. This sentiment, more than anything else, is the obstacle in the way of a third-term candidature. In the period immediately following Washington's death his memory was

[1] From a letter quoted in John Bigelow's *Retrospections of an Active Life*, vol. v. p. 167.

not thus sacrosanct. The echo of the abusive epithets with which some of his political opponents had vilified him had scarcely died away. Evidently, if Jefferson had been willing to undertake a third term he would have encountered no opposition on the ground that he was setting himself up to be a greater than Washington. But the passing of the years has made of the first President a heroic figure, whose unique stature it would to-day be almost *lèse majesté* to diminish even by implication. Professor Thayer's inference from the frequent re-election of State Governors therefore loses its point. You may re-elect a State Governor a dozen times without casting any reflection on the dignity of George Washington.

As long as this sentiment retains its strength, any aspirant for a third term, however personally popular, will be heavily handicapped even in the attempt to secure a nomination. But it would be rash to say that the difficulty he would have to overcome would amount to more than a handicap. The usage, if usage it be, is not so firmly established as absolutely to deter an ambitious man from making the venture. So glittering a prize offers a temptation that a people's favourite will rarely have the fortitude to resist, although, years earlier, he may have expressed his approval of the principle of rotation in office or even have declared his intention of being content with a second term. (Casca's story of how Cæsar thrice refused the crown comes irresistibly to mind when one is reading recent American history. ' Then he put it by again ; but, to my thinking, he was very loath to lay his fingers off it.') And a party convention that shared his own estimate of his popularity—a convention that believed it would win the election if it chose him as its candidate and lose it with any other nominee—might naturally take whatever risk was involved in furthering his aspirations.

In any event there can be very few opportunities of putting the alleged usage to the test. Most of the other usages noted in this book are being illustrated from day to day in the ordinary routine of government, and an occasion for the trial of their validity might occur at any moment. But amid the ups and downs of party politics in the United States it can only be seldom that the career of a President offers material for a study of this subject. And it is possible that before long the question will be definitely settled by the adoption of a Constitutional Amendment limiting the tenure of the Presidency to a single term.

V

THE PRESIDENT'S CABINET

IF a copy of the Fundamental Law of the American Constitution were placed in the hands of an intelligent foreigner who was entirely unacquainted with the political system of the United States, and he were asked to discover from it what group of men it provided as a body of advisers for the President, he would undoubtedly fix upon the Senate. It is by and with the advice and consent of the Senate that the President is to conclude treaties and to make all principal appointments to public offices. In such matters consultation with the Senate is compulsory. With one exception, to be presently mentioned, the Chief Executive is left in everything else to follow his own judgment. No advisory body other than the Senate is mentioned or suggested from beginning to end of the instrument.

Actually the custom of the Presidential office has developed in a manner not contemplated by the Constitution of 1787. Although the consent of the Senate is still required for the ratification of treaties and for official appointments, the President never meets the Senate in personal consultation, while he confers regularly with a body of advisers whose existence is not recognized anywhere in the Fundamental Law. Usage has destroyed the practice of conference with the Senate and has created the Cabinet.

In the nature of things it was inevitable that the President should gather around himself, regularly or irregularly, some group of political advisers. No man entrusted with such responsibilities could plough his furrow alone. Even despotic monarchs have felt the necessity of surrounding themselves with some sort of council to discuss and supplement their own schemes of government. The question was carefully considered in the 1787 Convention.[1] At that time, we must remember, the English Cabinet was as yet in a primitive stage, and the only English precedent available for the guidance of the American statesmen was the institution of the King in Council. Nearer at hand was the example of the State Governors' councils in colonial days. Various proposals for a Council of State were discussed and rejected by the Convention. One objection raised against such an institution was that an able council would thwart the President, while he would shelter himself under the sanction of a weak one. In his chapter on the subject in the *Federalist* (No. 69) Hamilton argued against a council not only on general principles but from the unsatisfactory working of councils in the State governments, and concluded:

[1] It will save many particular references if I acknowledge here, once for all, my debt, on all matters relating to the Cabinet, to Mr. Henry Barrett Learned's treatise on *The President's Cabinet*, first published in 1912, and to his paper, 'Some Aspects of the Cabinet Meeting,' read before the Columbia Historical Society of Washington, D.C., in 1914.

'A council to a magistrate, who is himself responsible for what he does, are generally nothing better than a clog upon his good intentions ; are often the instruments and accomplices of his bad ; and are almost always a cloak to his faults.'

But while the Fundamental Law, as finally drafted by the Convention, contained no suggestion of an advisory council, other than in its provisions for consultation with the Senate, it supplied the President with a limited and specialized opportunity of obtaining assistance in solving the problems of his administration. 'He may require,' runs Article II., 'the opinion, in writing, of the principal officer in each of the executive departments, upon any subject relating to the duties of their respective offices.' There is here, it will be noted, no thought of any meeting of the heads of departments, or even of any contribution by them of written expressions of individual opinion on matters of general policy. And it was left entirely to the discretion of the President himself whether he should seek the particular advice which he was thus authorized to obtain. The reason for stipulating for written opinions from the principal officers, as given by James Iredell, one of the members of the Convention, was that 'the necessity of their opinions being in writing will render them more cautious in giving them, and make them responsible should they give advice manifestly improper.'

At the outset the intentions of the framers of the Fundamental Law were faithfully carried out, as regards both a personal consultation of the Senate by the President and the requisition of written opinions from the heads of departments. George Washington appeared twice in the chamber of the Senate in 1789 to advise with its members in the matter of a proposed treaty with the Southern Indians. These first attempts at mutual conference were so unsatisfactory—the Senate being embarrassed by the great man's presence and the President himself becoming irritated by its proposal to refer to a committee the explanatory papers presented by his Secretary of War, whom he had brought with him—that neither the first nor any subsequent President ever again visited the Capitol for such a purpose. Even if the practice of personally consulting the Senate had not been brought to a speedy end by the incident of the Indian treaty it would inevitably have broken down sooner or later owing to the increase in the size of that body. The Senate in Washington's time was not much larger than some recent English Cabinets, and there could be no mechanical difficulty in his holding a real conference with a group of that size. It would be quite another thing to attempt to talk things over with ninety-six Senators.

Senator Lodge points out that one of the rules of the Senate still contemplates the possibility of visits from the President for the consideration of executive business—it gives instructions as to where he shall sit on such occasions—and remarks that, although it is never put into practical operation, it has importance not merely as embodying an unbroken tradition but as a formal recognition of certain constitutional principles of very great moment.

> ' By this rule,' he says, ' are recognized the right of the President to consult personally with the Senate, the position of the Senators as the President's only constitutional advisers, and the equality of the Senate in the conduct of all executive business in which, under the Constitution, they are entitled to share. The right of the President personally to consult the Senate as a body involves also the correlative right of the Senate, in the language of the Constitution, to advise the President. To the Senate alone is given this right to advise the Executive.'[1]

Of course; just as other rules that have fallen into desuetude formally recognize ' certain constitutional principles of very great moment '—just as, for instance, it is possible to interpret the continuance of the formalities of the Electoral system as a re-affirmation by the mass of the American people, every four years, of their belief in the traditional doctrine of their own incapacity to choose a fit person as President. But the rule has in practice become a dead letter, and, as no repetition of George Washington's experiment would ever be attempted to-day, we are surely entitled to regard this as one of the instances in which usage has over-ridden the intentions of the Fundamental Law.

Let us now turn to the question of the institution that has grown out of the article authorizing the President to obtain written advice from ' the principal

[1] H. C. Lodge, *A Frontier Town and Other Essays*, ed. 1906, p. 71.

officer in each of the executive departments.' The number and character of the executive departments have always been decided by Congress. Originally there were three—State, Treasury, and War. The Attorney-General was counted among the President's advisers from the first, although the Department of Justice, of which he is now the head, was not created until 1870. He was admitted to the group as the legal adviser to the President. The next department to be established was the Post Office, which dates from 1789. It was not, however, until 1829 that the Postmaster-General was considered a Presidential adviser. The innovation was made by President Jackson on his own initiative, without any recommendation from Congress. There were subsequently added to the list the Secretaryships of the Navy (1798), the Interior (1849), Agriculture (1889), and Commerce and Labour (1903). The last of these was divided in 1913 into two separate departments.

The first President availed himself constantly of the opportunity of requiring written opinions from the heads of the executive departments separately with respect to the affairs of their own offices.

'Washington,' writes Professor J. A. Woodburn, 'generally pursued the practice of consulting his Cabinet members individually. Before making up his mind what policy he should pursue, he asked the opinions of his secretaries in writing. Some of our most valuable historical State papers came to us in this way—in the written opinions of Jefferson and Hamilton prepared at Washington's request.

Note especially the opinions on our neutrality policy and the constitutionality of the first United States bank.'[1]

But later Presidents soon came to discard the method provided by the Fundamental Law. According to Mr. Learned, ' it has been generally true, since Washington's day, that written opinions have been exceptional as a mode of taking advice.' ' I have never,' wrote President Polk in 1848, ' called for any written opinions from my Cabinet, preferring to take their opinions after a discussion in Cabinet and in presence of each other. In this way harmony of opinion is more likely to exist.' The practice, however, was occasionally revived by Lincoln, especially in cases—such as frequently arose during the Civil War—that involved difficult technical points.

The quotation from Polk shows that, by his time at any rate, the practice of holding Cabinet meetings had become a well-established institution. It had begun as early as the first Presidency. Mr. Learned tells us that the first recorded consultation that was essentially a Cabinet meeting was held in April, 1791. Curiously enough, it took place in the absence of the President himself. He was away from the capital on a tour in the South, and had asked the heads of departments to hold such a meeting in case administrative business made it desirable. He requested further that the Vice-President should be asked to attend. In 1792 there are several clear records of Cabinet meetings, and in 1793 they became frequent.

[1] J. A. Woodburn, *The American Republic and its Government*, 2nd edition, p. 190.

The first known use of the word 'Cabinet' to denote the group of officers called into consultation by the President was made by Madison in the latter year. It appeared for the first time in a Supreme Court decision in 1803 and in a Presidential message to Congress in 1829. The first—and, as far as I can learn, the only—instance of its use in a statute occurred in 1907, when an appropriation bill introduced into Congress proposed certain changes in the salary of the heads of executive departments who were 'members of the President's Cabinet.' In the course of the debates exception was taken to the use of a term hitherto unknown to statute law, but, as it designated what had long been a recognized institution, no alteration was made in the text of the bill.

The Congressional precisians who objected to any mention of the Cabinet in a statute must have forgotten that you cannot make a thing disappear by refusing to give it a name. For generations the existence of a Cabinet had already been accepted as a matter of course in American politics. In the discussions that had taken place years before respecting the creation of new executive departments, the advocates of the change had laid stress not only upon the necessity of the proposed departments in themselves but upon the desirability of giving the interests affected a spokesman in the group of officers which administered the general government. A department that was represented in the Cabinet, it was argued, had a great advantage over a mere bureau in influencing the policies of the executive. So, too, when Commerce and Labour obtained recognition in 1903, one reason urged for combining them in a single department was that the creation of two new departments would have unduly increased the size of the Cabinet. Whenever a new President takes office the public judgment on the character of his appointments is always affected by a consideration of the quality of the new Cabinet as a corporate body, not merely as a collection of individuals severally responsible for the affairs of their own departments only. Thus, in 1921, Mr. Harding was congratulated on securing the assistance of Mr. Hoover, not simply because Mr. Hoover was believed to be a capable person to superintend the Department of Commerce, but because of the strength that would be brought to the Administration in its handling of international problems by the presence at the Cabinet table of a man who was so exceptionally qualified to advise on the relation of the United States to European affairs. So far, indeed, has the Cabinet meeting come to be recognized as part of the normal and essential machinery of government that, during the period immediately after President Wilson's breakdown when he was unable to attend to any business, no less than twenty-five Cabinet meetings were held in his absence, in order to ' instil confidence in the country that the government was functioning.' [1]

Nevertheless this body, although to-day making a regular contribution to the effective working of the

[1] David Lawrence, *The True Story of Woodrow Wilson*, ed. 1924, p. 285.

American Constitution, still remains unknown to its Fundamental Law. 'The Cabinet' says Mr. Taft, 'is a mere creation of the President's will. It is an extra-statutory and extra-constitutional body. It exists only by custom. If the President desired to dispense with it, he could do so.'[1] As Professor J. W. Burgess puts it :

> 'These officers ... certainly have no *collegiate* existence under the Constitution. The President may, if he chooses, consult them as a body, unless they themselves object. Should they object, he could not point to any specific clause in the Constitution which requires such an organization, or which authorizes him to require opinions in such a form.... What we call the Cabinet is, therefore, a purely voluntary, extra-legal association of the heads of the executive departments with the President, which may be dispensed with at any moment by the President, and whose resolutions do not legally bind the President in the slightest degree. They form a privy council, but not a ministry.'[2]

It is significant that whereas we hear of the Federal Executive, we never hear of the Federal Cabinet, or of the American Cabinet, or of the Cabinet of the United States. It is always the President's Cabinet. In the eyes of the law the President's conference with the heads of departments twice a week has no higher status than the interview he is accustomed to give to the Washington newspaper correspondents immediately afterward. Not only is the President

[1] W. H. Taft, *Our Chief Magistrate and his Powers*, ed. 1916, p. 30.
[2] J. W. Burgess, *Political Science and Constitutional Law*, ed. 1891, vol. ii. p. 263.

free either to call them together or not to call them, but he is equally free to invite whom he will to the meeting. We have seen that the Postmaster-General was ignored for forty years, and was then admitted by the exercise of the President's own discretion. So, too, quite recently President Harding enlarged the meeting by inviting the Vice-President to attend it. In so doing he reverted to a precedent set by Washington at that first Cabinet meeting in 1791. Mr. Learned, however, writing in 1912, reported that up to that time there had been known no subsequent instance of the attendance of a Vice-President, although some Presidents had occasionally consulted Vice-Presidents privately on specific questions of policy. Clearly, if the Fundamental Law had definitely prescribed the holding of a conference of heads of departments, the Vice-President, not being of their number, would not have been eligible for admission to it.

If the President desired to dispense with the Cabinet, he could do so, says Mr. Taft. Could he? Technically, of course, he could, but whether any President, however personally popular, would be able to break away from the tradition of 130 years is never likely to be tested. One cannot imagine that any newly-elected President would nowadays omit to call the executive chiefs in consultation but content himself with asking their opinions in writing on departmental affairs—keeping them, so to speak, in separate cubby-holes like the leader-writers of *The Times* under Delane's editorship. Usage has made the common practice virtually as binding as though it were an instruction set down in black and white in the Fundamental Law. It is a fairly safe prediction that to this Cabinet meeting future Presidents will continue to summon the heads of departments only. An invitation to the Vice-President will not become a corollary to the accepted usage, for it was found that the enlargement of the meeting in 1921 was of doubtful advantage. It is true that, when Vice-President Coolidge was called to the head of the table by Mr. Harding's death, it was generally remarked that his participation in the sessions of the Cabinet during the last year and a half would now prove of great service to him, inasmuch as it would have already acquainted him at first hand with the recent history of the questions that his own administration would have to deal with. But such an argument is two-edged, as became evident when certain scandals in the Harding Administration were brought to light, and it became necessary, in order to keep the new President from association with such a discredited régime, to take the view that his attendance at Cabinet meetings did not really mean anything. Before his election to the Vice-Presidency in 1924 Gen. C. G. Dawes emphatically expressed the opinion that it was unwise for the occupant of that office to sit with the Cabinet, and after his election the experiment was not repeated.

VI

THE CABINET AND CONGRESS

ONE of the many contrasts with Parliament that strike the attention of an English visitor to Congress is the lack of a Treasury Bench. No Cabinet ministers sit in either House. They are excluded by an article of the Fundamental Law of the Constitution which provides that ' no person holding any office under the United States shall be a member of either House during his continuance in office.' For a few years there was a similar prohibition in England. The Act of Settlement of 1701 ordained that ' no person who has an office or place of profit under the King, or receives a pension from the Crown, shall be capable of serving as a member of the House of Commons.' Hence the expedient of appointment to the Stewardship of the Chiltern Hundreds as a convenient substitute for any legal means of resignation. As far as Cabinet ministers were concerned the restriction was repealed by an Act of 1705, which excluded from Parliament certain specified classes of office-holders and provided that a member who accepted office under the Crown must be re-elected in order to retain his seat.

But while the Fundamental Law denies to the heads of the executive departments the right to be members of Congress, it places no embargo upon their personal presence on the floor of either House or their participation in debates relating to the affairs of their departments. Accordingly, the Act of 1789, which established the Treasury Department, provided that 'the Secretary of the Treasury shall make report and give information to either branch of the legislature in person or in writing, as may be required, respecting all matters referred to him by the Senate or the House of Representatives, or which shall appertain to his office.' In January, 1790, the first Secretary of the Treasury, Alexander Hamilton, was called upon to present to the House of Representatives his 'Report on the Public Credit,' which he had prepared at its request. He was ready, and indeed desirous, to present it in person, but Congress decided, after debate, that it should be communicated in writing. The ostensible reason for this preference was that the details of the report were so numerous and intricate that, delivered orally, they would not remain in the memory of his hearers, but what really determined the decision of Congress was its fear of Hamilton's superiority as a debater over any of its own members, coupled with a certain instinctive apprehension of executive encroachment upon its own authority and influence. On a later occasion an attempt was made by certain members of the House, but was prevented by the objection of the majority, to secure the presence of Hamilton and Knox, the Secretary of War, at a discussion of the failure of St. Clair's expedition against the Indians.

THE HAMILTON PRECEDENT

The precedent set in the reception of Hamilton's report has prevailed until this day. All subsequent official reports of the heads of departments have been communicated in writing. Usage, and usage alone, prohibits Cabinet ministers from speech or presence on the floor of either House except on some purely ceremonial occasion, as, for instance, when the Secretary of State recently addressed a combined session of both Houses at a Harding memorial service. The embargo does not extend to appearances before Congressional committees, which frequently request the head of the department within whose province the subject under consideration falls to assist them by giving evidence. He may use his own discretion, however, as to whether he shall consent or refuse to attend the committee hearings. On February 9, 1923, for example, Mr. Hughes, then Secretary of State, declined to comply with a request from the Foreign Relations Committee of the Senate that he should appear before them and explain the activities of the unofficial representatives of the United States serving with the Reparation Commission. He had already, he said, given adequate information in the written communications sent to the committee, and he could not make the matter clearer in any oral explanations.

The effect of the exclusion of Cabinet officers from membership of Congress does not require consideration here, as that prohibition is imposed by the Fundamental Law. The results of the usage which prevents a minister from reporting in person on departmental business are of less consequence, but are important enough to deserve attention. Mr. Learned acutely remarks that it has circumscribed the positions of the secretaries in such a way as to make them regard themselves as essentially belonging to the Executive, and has thus helped to unify the President and his personal advisers. Its other effects are more obvious and conspicuous. For one thing, it has greatly hampered the work of legislation. Bills pass through all their stages in both Houses while containing defects which would have been remedied if the head of one of the executive departments could have been brought into consultation. As things now are, an error that would render a measure unworkable may not be discovered until it is pointed out by the President in his veto message. Mr. Taft has said that ' the time lost in Congress over useless discussions of issues that might be disposed of by a single statement from the head of a department, no one can appreciate unless he has filled such a place.'[1]

Even more, perhaps, does this usage make against efficiency of administration. The lack of such an institution as the ' question time ' of the British Parliament is a serious disadvantage to the American Government. At home the daily interrogation of ministers is sometimes criticized as a waste of time and labour, but no one would ever say another word against it who was familiar with the working of the American system. The possibility of ' questions in

[1] W. H. Taft, *Our Chief Magistrate and his Powers*, ed. 1916, p. 31.

the House' is an invaluable safeguard of competence and integrity in the executive departments. No less an authority than Woodrow Wilson once expressed the opinion that

> 'we should have not a little light thrown daily, and often when it is least expected, upon the conduct of the departments, if the heads of the departments had daily to face the representatives of the people, to propose, defend, explain administrative policy, upon the floor of the Houses, ... and heads of departments would be happy under such a system only when they were very straightforward and honest and able men.'[1]

When the naval oil reserves scandals were exposed in the winter of 1923-24 it was pointed out that no such conditions could ever have developed if Cabinet officers had been liable to be periodically questioned in Congress respecting the affairs of their departments. The acts that afterward aroused such general disapprobation would have had to run the gauntlet of criticism in Congress as soon as they were known, or even suspected, to be in contemplation, and the inquiries made would have balked the whole project. Indeed, the mere certainty that Congress would want to know all about it would probably have deterred the ministers concerned from attempting anything of the kind.

While the legislature thus lacks any normal and regular means of learning what is going on in the departments, it is by no means debarred from dis-

---

[1] From an address to the Virginia State Bar Association, delivered on August 3, 1897, and quoted by Professor H. J. Ford in *Woodrow Wilson, the Man and his Work*, p. 97.

cussing departmental business. A Congressman is at perfect liberty to deliver a speech in which he roundly denounces the conduct of a particular Cabinet officer by name. But the man whom he assails is not there to present his own case. When Freeman visited Washington in 1882 and attended a Congressional debate, there was one incident that 'specially struck' him. 'One representative,' he reports, 'made a fierce attack on the Secretary of the Navy, and the Secretary of the Navy was not there to defend himself.'[1] Anyone who visited the Senate early in 1924 might have been present at a precisely similar scene. There was introduced into that body, and ultimately carried after several days' discussion, a resolution condemning the conduct of the Secretary of the Navy and calling upon the President to dismiss him. If a similar attack were made in Parliament, the incriminated minister would, of course, have full opportunity of meeting his accusers face to face. But during the whole of this long debate neither the Secretary himself nor any of his colleagues had any chance of saying a word in his defence. The most that he could do was to issue statements to the press, and to prime friendly Senators privately with arguments that might be used in his favour.

Except for the presentation of the annual reports there is no authorized machinery for keeping the Legislature acquainted with what is happening in the executive departments. Individual Congressmen

[1] E. A. Freeman, *Some Impressions of the United States*, p. 119.

INVESTIGATING COMMITTEES

who are interested in some particular subject are left to make such explorations of the unknown territory as they can, sometimes getting tips from the newspaper correspondents at the capital—as a class, the best-informed men in the United States about the work of the government as a whole—and sometimes picking up scraps of information from visits to the departmental offices, where their inquiries probably put the officials to scarcely less trouble than would be involved in preparing answers to 'questions in the House.' If any suspicion arises as to the conduct of a Government department, the only method available to Congress for getting at the facts is the passing of a resolution authorizing an inquiry by one of its committees—either a standing committee or a special committee of investigation appointed for the purpose. The department concerned inevitably regards the institution of such an inquiry as an attack upon it, and its attitude toward the investigation is tinged with a resentment, not to say hostility, which disposes it to reveal as little as it may. The proceedings, indeed, tend as a whole to take on a sensational character, and one is not surprised to find that Mr. Walter Lippmann, though writing some time before the episodes of the spring of 1924, could speak of 'that legalized atrocity, the Congressional investigation, where Congressmen, starved of their legitimate food for thought, go on a wild and feverish man-hunt, and do not stop at cannibalism.'[1] At best the holding of an investi-

[1] Walter Lippman, *Public Opinion*, ed. 1922, p. 289.

gation of this kind is a clumsy, tedious, and costly [1] method of getting at the truth. It may drag on for an unconscionable period—determined, perhaps, by the exigencies of an election campaign—and the resulting report may not be presented until after so long an interval that the public has lost all interest in the subject.

It is little wonder that attempts have been made from time to time to break down a usage which is admitted to have such unfortunate consequences. In 1881 a select committee of the Senate, composed of Republicans and Democrats in equal numbers, reported unanimously in favour of a bill providing that the heads of the executive departments should be entitled to seats on the floor of each House of Congress, with the right to participate in debate on matters relating to the business of their respective departments. They were further to attend in the Senate on Tuesdays and Fridays and in the House on Mondays and Thursdays, at the opening of the sessions, in order to give information asked by resolution or in reply to questions of which three days' notice had been given. Their participation in the debates was to be optional, but their attendance to give information would be compulsory. No attempt, however, was made to carry this recom-

---

[1] For the fiscal year 1924 an appropriation of $100,000 was made to meet the expenses of investigations ordered by the Senate. Before that body had been in session for three months it notified the House Committee on appropriations that this sum had been exhausted and an additional sum of $125,000 was needed to meet expenses already incurred. By April 16 the actual expenditure had amounted to $325,000.

PROPOSALS FOR REFORM

mendation into effect.[1] President Taft, in his annual message to Congress on December 19, 1912, urged the necessity of a reform of this kind, but once more nothing was done. In 1924 proposals similar to those of 1881 were considered in committees of both Houses. It has been pointed out, in support of such a measure, that the presence of non-members and their participation in debates would be no innovation, as similar privileges, without the right of voting, are already accorded in the House of Representatives to delegates from the territories of Alaska and Hawaii and to ' resident commissioners ' from the Philippines and Porto Rico. There are precedents, too, outside the American Union, for the granting of such opportunities to Cabinet ministers. The Constitution of the Southern Confederacy contained the provision that ' Congress may, by law, grant to the principal officer in each of the executive departments a seat upon the floor of either House, with the privilege of discussing any measures appertaining to his department.' The principle that ministers, while being members of one House of a bi-cameral Legislature, may speak in either is in force in Italy and has been adopted in the recently-created Constitution of Northern Ireland. Under the Constitution of the Irish Free State it is not necessary for the whole body of ministers to be members of either House of Parliament, but all

[1] The greater part of the text of this report is printed in an appendix to H. J. Ford's *The Rise and Growth of American Politics*, and is also given by Gamaliel Bradford in *The Lesson of Popular Government*, vol. ii. pp. 324 *et seqq.*

ministers have the right of speech in the Chamber of Deputies.[1]

The adoption of such a scheme would undoubtedly remedy those defects of the present system that have been noted above. It would have far-reaching consequences in other directions. Mr. Taft believes that it 'would impose on the President greater difficulty in selecting his Cabinet and would lead him to prefer men of legislative experience who have shown their power to take care of themselves in legislative debate.' It would also 'give the President what he ought to have, some direct initiative in legislation and an opportunity through the presence of his competent representatives in Congress to keep each House advised of the facts in the actual operation of the government.'[2] It would not be rash to predict that it would bring about a radical change in the normal process of legislation. The proceedings of the standing committees would soon come to mean less and debates on the floor of the House to mean more. The report of the Senate committee of 1881, replying to the objection that it would impose an additional burden upon ministers already over-worked, anticipated that the carrying out of this reform would make it necessary for them to be relieved of attention to harassing detail and would compel the appointment of larger and more competent staffs. It would thus be 'the first step towards a sound Civil Service reform' which would

[1] See Professor Herbert A. Smith, *Federalism in N. America*, pp. 40, 246.
[2] W. H. Taft, *Our Chief Magistrate and his Powers*, ed. 1916, p. 31.

'secure a larger wisdom in the adoption of policies and a better system in their execution.'

These would be substantial gains, and it is not surprising that proposals of this kind should be warmly supported by men who have had first-hand experience of the difficulties of administration under the present system. Mr. Bradford quotes to that effect several Cabinet ministers who have discussed the matter with him in private conversation.[1] One of them was a former Secretary of the Treasury, who declared that he would never again accept a Cabinet office without an opportunity of speaking in Congress. The bills introduced in 1924 similarly elicited several expressions of approval from members of Mr. Coolidge's Cabinet. But the very reasons which commend the scheme to Cabinet ministers tend to discredit it in the eyes of members of the Legislature. Mr. Taft's prediction that it would give the President some direct initiative in legislation is alone enough to alarm a Congress that is always jealous of executive encroachments upon its own power. The additional prestige and influence that it would bestow upon Cabinet ministers would be equally unwelcome at the Capitol. At present a seat in the Senate is more highly coveted than most Cabinet offices. Under the proposed scheme, with the departments administered by men of more distinguished reputation, who would figure more prominently in the public eye and would enjoy

[1] Gamaliel Bradford, *The Lesson of Popular Government*, ed. 1899, vol. ii. p. 411.

greater opportunities of promoting their policies, membership of the Cabinet would become one of the most attractive prizes of a political career, and a seat in the Senate would correspondingly depreciate in value. It is significant that the provision in the Constitution of the Confederacy which gave the Confederate Congress the right to bring itself into closer co-operative relations with the Executive by granting seats, with the privilege of debate, to the heads of the departments, was a dead letter. The innovation had been actually practised under the provisional government of 1861, but after the formal Constitution came into operation the Legislature never availed itself of this opportunity of personal contact with Cabinet officers. ' This wise and judicious provision,' says the President of the Confederacy, ' which would have tended to obviate much delay and misunderstanding, was never put into execution by the necessary legislation.'[1]

An observer may reasonably doubt whether any attempt to bring to an end the present isolation of the executive from the legislative branch of the government, without impairing their mutual independence, would really be successful. Would the proposed change fit in harmoniously with the American political system? The presence of Cabinet ministers in Parliament, in order to answer questions and take part in debates, is a natural and essential feature of a system which gives the Cabinet a direct

[1] Jefferson Davis, *The Rise and Fall of the Confederate Government*, ed. 1881, vol. i. p. 259.

responsibility for legislation and makes its retention of office dependent upon a vote of the House of Commons. The close association of the Cabinet with the Legislature is part of the very framework of the English system. If American ministers, however, were to appear periodically in the Senate and the House for the purposes suggested, they would still be responsible not to Congress but to the President. They would remain 'chief clerks, responsible to the President, appointed and dismissed by him at pleasure. Nothing that Congress might do could compel their dismissal, nothing that they themselves could do would force a dissolution of Congress and an appeal to the country.'[1] The innovation, though not conflicting in the slightest degree with the letter of the Fundamental Law, would be entirely alien to its spirit. It would really be incompatible with the political doctrine on which the mutual relations of the American executive and the American legislature are based. It would mean the sewing of a new and discordant patch upon an old garment. You cannot enjoy at the same time the advantages of the separation between executive and legislative functions which characterizes the American plan of government and the union of them which is a cardinal feature of the English system.

[1] W. MacDonald, *A New Constitution for a New America*, ed. 1923, p. 47.

VII

APPOINTMENT AND REMOVAL

THE Fundamental Law of the American Constitution is, on the whole, remarkably free from ambiguities and inconsistencies, but on one question of great importance its meaning was left doubtful. The President, it ordained,

> 'shall nominate, and by and with the advice and consent of the Senate shall appoint, ambassadors, other public ministers and consuls, judges of the Supreme Court, and all other officers of the United States whose appointments are not herein otherwise provided for, and which shall be established by law: but the Congress may by law vest the appointment of such inferior officers as they think proper in the President alone, in the courts of law, or in the heads of departments.'

If the words 'advice and' had been omitted from this article it would have been clear that the Senate had nothing to do with any appointment until the President asked its approval of a selection he had already made. The function of nomination is expressly mentioned as his, and his alone. But if the Senate is not only to give its 'consent' before the proposed appointment is finally made but is also to give its 'advice,' its share in the transaction must evidently begin at an earlier stage. It cannot advise as to the filling of a vacant post without taking

THE SAVANNAH CASE 127

part in the suggestion of names of candidates and thus depriving the President of the exclusive power of nomination.

Historically, it seems to be clear that the members of the 1787 Convention intended the initative to lie entirely with the President. ' There will, of course,' wrote Hamilton in the *Federalist* (No. 65), ' be no exertion of choice on the part of the Senate. They may defeat one choice of the executive and compel him to make another, but they cannot themselves choose—they can only ratify or reject the choice of the President.' The same interpretation is implied in No. 75, where he argues that the necessity of concurrence by the Senate will ' be an excellent check upon a spirit of favouritism in the President,' and will ' tend greatly to preventing the appointment of unfit characters from State prejudice, from family connection, from personal attachment, or from a view to popularity.'

The first clash between the two authorities took place early in the history of the new Constitution. Taking to heart the lesson of his abortive conference with the Senate respecting the Indian treaty, George Washington made no attempt to seek the advice of that body concerning any of his appointments, but sent in his nominations for confirmation or rejection. In 1789 the Senate refused to endorse his nomination to the post of naval officer at the port of Savannah. It gave him no statement of the grounds of its refusal. The President replied with a special message, in which he defended the fitness of his choice.

'Permit me,' he suggested further, 'to submit to your consideration whether, on occasions where the propriety of nominations appears questionable to you, it would not be expedient to communicate that circumstance to me, and thereby avail yourself of the information which led me to make them, and which I would with pleasure lay before you.'

He avoided further contention, however, by making a new nomination, which was approved.[1]

In the Savannah incident the reason for the Senate's refusal was an objection raised by the two Senators from Georgia, in which State Savannah is situated. That objection was of great significance, for it pointed the way to a compromise which usage has established as a constitutional practice. It would obviously be inconvenient for a President to send nominations to the Senate on a 'hit or miss' system, without knowing beforehand whether they would be acceptable or how many times he might have to revise them before the necessary consent was obtained. On the other hand, it would be impracticable for him to take the whole body of the Senate into consultation before offering a name in the first place. The risk of a deadlock is minimized by his consulting informally with the Senators from the State in which the office lies, if they are members of his own political party. Actually this amounts in most instances to his taking the advice of these two Senators as to a selection. A nomination approved by them is practically certain of final confirmation

[1] See H. J. Ford, *The Rise and Growth of American Politics*, ed. 1898, p. 260.

by the Senate as a whole. The arrangement is a 'log-rolling' one, which has been dignified by the name of 'Senatorial courtesy.' 'If you will help me to get the appointments I want in my State, I will help you to get the appointments you want in your State.'

It is only the more important appointments within a State that are thus determined. For the lesser posts, notably the postmasterships in the smaller cities and towns, the President depends for suggestions not upon its Senators but upon its delegates in the House of Representatives.

'It has become a settled custom,' writes Professor C. A. Beard, ' to allow the representative, if he is of the President's party, to name the appointees of his district [*Anglice*, constituency]; but if he is not of the President's party the patronage goes to the Senator or Senators. Mr. Bristow, the Fourth Assistant Postmaster-General, recently testified that when there was a vacancy in a post office the administration in power would send a request, upon a printed blank, to the member representing the district, if he was in political sympathy with the President's party, asking for the recommendation of some one to fill the place.'[1]

The right of Congressmen to share in the distribution of these spoils is recognized as superior to that which can be claimed by the most influential leaders of the party outside Congress. Thus, in his biography of Mark Hanna, Mr. Herbert Croly mentions a controversy in 1890 when Hanna was backing a candidate for the Cleveland postmastership against

[1] C. A. Beard, *The American Government and Politics*, ed. 1915, p. 191.

the candidate of Representative T. E. Burton. 'President Harrison insisted that Mr. Burton, as the local Congressman, was entitled to the appointment; and he received it.'[1] A more recent instance is thus reported in the *Washington Post* of April 12, 1924:

> 'The question whether members of Congress or State officials shall decide postmaster appointments was decided in favour of the former yesterday by President Coolidge in appointing a postmaster at Duluth, Minn. Representative Larson (Republican), whose district includes Duluth, recommended reappointment of Thomas Considine, who received his original commission from President Wilson. Gov. Preus recommended W. C. Sargent, the other man on the eligible list, and made a special trip to Washington last week to urge the appointment. Mr. Coolidge sent the nomination of Considine to the Senate.'

There is usually an understanding between the Senators and Congressmen from a State as to how this patronage is to be divided between them, but occasionally there is a conflict of appetites. Mr. John D. Long, Secretary of the Navy in M'Kinley's first administration, recorded in his journal the following curious incident:

> 'Senator Penrose comes in, and we came near striking fire about a little twopenny appointment of shipkeeper at $2 a day at the Philadelphia Navy Yard. Representative Butler wants it, and Penrose wants it. It is like a fight of wolves over a carcass. Shameful and disgracing picture: that a Senator of the United States should be running his legs off, wasting his time, when great questions

---

[1] Herbert Croly, *Marcus Alonzo Hanna*, ed. 1912, p. 154.

AN INGENIOUS DEFENCE

are at stake, about this carrion of patronage—which very patronage only hurts instead of helping his political prospects.'[1]

As in this instance, appointments to many minor offices are virtually made by the head of the department concerned, and only indirectly by the President.

The practice which has thus become part of the usage of the Constitution has been ingeniously defended as a virtual fulfilment of the Fundamental Law.

'Nothing is more inept,' remarks Senator Lodge, 'than to criticize a President because he consults the Senators from a State in regard to an appointment in or from that State. The Senators are his constitutional advisers. In some way he must consult them, and it is impossible that any President should be able to know enough about the men in forty-five States to enable him to appoint intelligently unless he could avail himself of the knowledge of those who represent the several States. The consultation of Senators by the President, therefore, in regard to appointments is nothing more than carrying out the intent of the Constitution in the manner which practice has shown to be the only convenient one.'[2]

The plea offered by this distinguished apologist for the prevailing practice was evidently intended for very uncritical readers. Even if his argument were valid as regards the consultation of Senators, it would not apply to the consultation of Representatives, whom the Fundamental Law does not recognize in the matter at all. They are not the President's

[1] *America of Yesterday*, edited by L. S. Mayo, ed. 1923, p. 156.
[2] H. C. Lodge, *A Frontier Town and Other Essays*, ed. 1906, p. 76.

132   APPOINTMENT AND REMOVAL

'constitutional advisers' in this or in anything else. And, as to the Senate, if the 'intent of the Constitution' were being faithfully carried out, the influence of Senators in making appointments would not be restricted, as it is to-day, to Senators belonging to the President's own party. If a Republican President is in office, the Democratic members of the Senate are just as much his 'constitutional advisers' as the Republican members. But he would never dream of seeking the advice of Senators from a Democratic State as to the appointments he should make within their constituency. In such a case the nominating power is virtually exercised by authorities unknown to the Fundamental Law. Mr. Croly thus describes the system introduced by Senator Hanna for appointing Federal officers in the Democratic South under the M'Kinley administration.

> 'The local offices were usually filled on the recommendation of the defeated Congressional candidate, and Mr. Hanna expected by the recognition of these leaders of forlorn hopes to induce a better quality of men to run for office. For the higher Federal offices, such as the United States Judges and Attorneys, the recommendations were usually accepted of a Board of Referees, consisting of the defeated candidate for Governor, the chairman of the State Committee, and the members of the National Committee from that State.'[1]

Not much of 'the intent of the Constitution' can be discerned there!

The President's patronage is one of his most valuable assets, as it enables him to traffic with

[1] *Op. cit.* p. 298.

THE PRESIDENT'S PATRONAGE

members of Congress for their support for the legislative measures he favours. According to a return of the Civil Service Commission quoted by Mr. Henry Litchfield West, a former Commissioner of the District of Columbia, there were on June 30, 1917, no less than 125,129 persons who came within the Presidential power of appointment, or who were directly or indirectly named by heads of departments selected by the President. This figure excludes employees selected by competitive examination and labourers engaged in Panama Canal work and elsewhere. The annual salaries paid to these appointed employees would certainly amount to $250,000,000.

> 'The spoils of office,' says Mr. West, 'which figured so largely in Andrew Jackson's administration were as a tiny rivulet compared with the mighty patronage of a President at the present time ... With the knowledge that the attitude of an administration toward his candidacy may make him or break him, few legislators dare to be *persona non grata* with a President of their political faith.'[1]

Mr. West quotes in this connection from a letter made public on September 15, 1910, signed by Charles D. Norton, then Secretary to President Taft. The writer of this letter stated that

> 'while certain legislation pending in Congress was opposed by certain Republicans, the President felt it to be his duty to his party and to the country to withhold Federal patronage from certain Senators and Congressmen who seemed to be in opposition to the administration's efforts to carry out the promises of the party platform.'[2]

[1] H. L. West, *Federal Power : Its Growth and Necessity*, ed. 1918, p. 154.
[2] *Op. cit.* p. 163.

At the same time their share in this power not only assists members of the legislature to build up a political 'machine' of their own in their States but enables them to exact a price for their co-operation in the legislative plans of the Executive.

> 'The exact relation,' says Professor C. E. Merriam, 'between the President and the Senators and Congressmen in the selection of these officials has never been determined, and must depend to a great extent on the relative strength and weakness of the officials concerned. A strong President or one closely interested in the placing of patronage will go much further in the actual choices that a weak President or one less concerned with the official list. Again, a President may prefer the passage of legislative projects which have come to be called "administration measures" to official appointments and may use his appointing power to secure the passage of laws otherwise difficult to obtain. There comes to be a process of jockeying between the Executive and the members of the legislative body, in which in dignified manner, of course, the relative merits of the law and the appointments are confirmed and appraised.'[1]

Mr. Roosevelt, on entering the White House, declared his own policy in these words: 'In the appointments I shall go on exactly as I did while I was Governor of New York. The Senators and Congressmen shall ordinarily name the men, but I shall name the standard, and the men have got to come up to it.'[2]

That, however, is more easily said than done.

[1] C. E. Merriam, *The American Party System*, ed. 1922, p. 345.
[2] J. B. Bishop, *Theodore Roosevelt and his Time*, ed. 1920, vol. i. p. 157.

A CONFLICT OF POWERS 135

And the mischief of the prevailing custom is enhanced when the preferences and prejudices of individual Senators come to sway the President's choice not only in making local appointments but in filling Federal offices of larger scope.

> 'The President,' says Professor James T. Young, 'must peddle out his appointments to the chief supporters of each Senator, or he must undertake a wearing and harassing struggle to urge the Senators to submit men really qualified for the service.... Countless instances are known in which men abundantly qualified for a national post of importance, who were acceptable to the President, have been quietly dropped out of consideration because they were for some reason not congenial to a Senator from their State.'[1]

No President of any marked individuality has escaped frequent clashes with the Senate as a whole, or at any rate with individual Senators of influence, over this matter of appointments. Even President Roosevelt found that the apparently practical compromise he enunciated as his guiding principle sometimes failed to work smoothly.[2]

A year ago anyone would have asserted, without fear of contradiction, that there was one class of offices in regard to which the President had obtained, through usage, an unfettered power not only of nomination but virtually of appointment also. He was allowed to use his own discretion in selecting the

[1] J. T. Young, *The New American Government and its Work*, ed. 1923, p. 31.
[2] See J. B. Bishop, *Theodore Roosevelt and his Time*, ed. 1920, vol. i. pp. 154, 235, 248, 442, and vol. ii. p. 14.

heads of departments, *i.e.*, the members of his Cabinet, and the confirmation of his choice by the Senate had become a mere formality. His independence in this respect might be regarded as, in some sense, a compensation for his deference to the wishes of Senators in the matter of other appointments. This group of officers constitutes what is popularly known as the President's ' official family,' and it was considered only reasonable that he should have a free hand in selecting the men who were to be his principal agents in the task of administration. The last instance of an actual refusal by the Senate to confirm a Cabinet nomination had occurred in 1868, when a name sent in by President Johnson for the Attorney-Generalship was rejected. In the following year President Grant withdrew his nomination of Mr. A. T. Stewart to be Secretary of the Treasury through receiving an intimation that it would not be confirmed by the Senate. It turned out that the President had overlooked the fact that Mr. Stewart, who was the head of a large department store in New York, would have had opportunities of using his control of the Treasury Department to promote his own interests as an importer, and was thus, by statute, ineligible for the post.

A test of the strength of this usage came in 1877, when the Senate deliberately broke away from the custom of confirming Cabinet nominations as a matter of course. In that year the entire list of President Hayes' proposed Cabinet was referred to committees for examination and report. At that

CABINET NOMINATIONS

time several of the most influential leaders of the Republican party occupied seats in the Senate, and they took this means of getting even with the new President for his omission to consult them in constructing his official ' slate.' But this departure from the conventional practice aroused such strong protests throughout the country that the committees to which the nominations had been referred hastened to report favourably on them, and within three days they had all been confirmed in the full Senate by an almost unanimous vote.[1]

The lesson seemed to have proved effective. No subsequent President, whether his own party was in control of the Senate or not, had to see his Cabinet nominations ' held up ' in this fashion—until 1925. In that year President Coolidge nominated Mr. Charles B. Warren for the post of Attorney-General. Strong objection was immediately raised in the Senate, but few people expected that it would prevail against a usage that appeared to be so firmly established. A typical press comment was that of the Washington correspondent of the *New Republic*, who, while himself opposed to the appointment, predicted that it would ' of course ' be confirmed.

' No one,' he said, ' can recall that the Senate ever rejected a Cabinet selection by the President. It is universally conceded the Executive has the right to select his own official family, and their submission to the Senate is merely a form.' [2]

[1] See J. W. Burgess, *The Administration of President Hayes*, ed. 1916, p. 66.

[2] T. R. B. in the *New Republic*, February 4, 1925.

When the votes were taken, however, on March 10, the nomination of Mr. Warren was rejected by forty-one to thirty-nine. Mr. Coolidge replied to this rebuff by sending in the same name a second time and by issuing from the White House a statement expressing the hope

> 'that the unbroken practice of three generations of permitting the President to choose his own Cabinet will not now be changed, and that the opposition to Mr. Warren, upon further consideration, will be withdrawn, in order that the country may have the benefit of his excellent qualities and the President may be unhampered in choosing his own method of executing the laws.'

He also declared his intention, in the event of a second rejection, of offering Mr. Warren a recess appointment as soon as the existing session came to an end, which would be within a few days. This appointment would be made in virtue of a provision of the Fundamental Law that 'the President shall have power to fill up all vacancies that may happen during the recess of the Senate, by granting commissions which shall expire at the end of their next session.' On March 16 the nomination of Mr. Warren was again rejected, this time by forty-six votes to thirty-nine. The deadlock was broken by Mr. Warren's refusal to accept the offer of a recess appointment. Thereupon the President sent to the Senate another name, which was at once approved.

On the face of it this incident might seem to have administered a death-blow to the commonly-accepted usage. But that conclusion would be premature.

THE ATTORNEY-GENERAL 139

The circumstances were exceptional. We must remember that, in the American political system, the Attorney-General fills a much more responsible rôle than in the English. He is not only the legal adviser of the Government, but he is also the head of the Department of Justice. He is charged with the selection, for nomination by the President, of the minor Federal judges, the district attorneys, the marshals and the other legal representatives of the Federal Government throughout the Union, and with seeing that their work is efficiently done. It is the duty of the Department of Justice to investigate all suspected violations of the Federal laws—smuggling, Post Office frauds, fraudulent bankruptcies, bucket shops, moonshining, and what not—and for this purpose it maintains an extensive secret service. The power of the Department to institute, or refrain from instituting, prosecutions under such an Act as the Sherman Anti-Trust Law is alone enough to make the choice of its head a matter deserving the most careful consideration.

> 'He possesses,' says the *New Republic*, 'enormous and increasing powers which to a large extent necessarily elude the supervision of his chief. An unfit selection ... may demoralize and poison the administration of justice within the whole area of Federal jurisdiction, and commit in the name of the law all kinds of mistakes and abuses.'[1]

At the moment when Mr. Warren's nomination was sent to the Senate there was good reasons for unusual vigilance. The omitted passage in the

[1] *New Republic*, in an editorial article, March 25, 1925.

above quotation from the *New Republic* specified certain recent occupants of the office as examples of ' an unfit selection.' Within the last few years the Department of Justice had been much under fire, and exposures made in the course of Senatorial investigations had aroused much concern in the public mind. In 1924 the difficulty of getting rid of an unworthy Attorney-General, who was ultimately dismissed by the President, had emphasized the importance of taking greater care about the appointment to that office in the first place. The Senate began to feel that it had been too easy-going in confirming any Cabinet nomination without question. As Senator Borah put it in the debates on the Warren nomination, ' things had happened ' which had aroused the Senate ' to the necessity of re-examining its duty and its obligation,' and which ' would be sufficient to justify the Senate in adopting a more rigid and more exacting and more determined rule in regard to their conduct in these matters.'

That was the situation when President Coolidge nominated to the Attorney-Generalship a lawyer who had been closely connected with a sugar trust that had been almost continuously under investigation for the last forty years, and that had just been charged by the Federal Trade Commission with engaging in a conspiracy in restraint of trade. Was it fitting, asked the opponents of the nomination, that a man with this record should be entrusted with the responsibility of administering the laws against business combinations ? One of them went

THE WARREN NOMINATION

so far as to declare that, in that event, the only consistent thing for Congress to do would be to wipe the Sherman Act off the statute-books. It will thus be seen that, in making such a nomination, Mr. Coolidge strained to the breaking point the obligation to respect the normal practice. He offered a vulnerable candidate at the very time when it was especially expedient to beware of presenting any name that would arouse suspicion. The leader of the attack in the Senate subscribed in principle to the theory that a President should name the members of his Cabinet without interference, but maintained that the requirement of confirmation by the Senate imposed upon that body the responsibility of preventing an improper appointment. Thus, the conflict between the President and the Senate was due not to any dissatisfaction with the general working of the usage but to the peculiar relations of this individual nominee to a question of paramount importance in the administration of the office to which he was nominated. According to the best-informed opinion in Washington, if the nomination of Mr. Warren had been made to any other place in the Cabinet except the Attorney-Generalship, even to the Secretaryship of State, it would have been confirmed without hesitation. It is significant that, as soon as his name was withdrawn and another was substituted for it, the President's second choice was promptly accepted. It was that of a personal friend of Mr. Coolidge's of whom little was known, but there was no delay in order to make any investigation of his fitness. Within four hours the new nomination had passed through all its stages of report by the Judiciary Committee and consideration in full session of the Senate.

We can no longer say, then, as could have been said a year before, that the President possesses undisputed control over appointments to his Cabinet. In such matters the Senate does not now shut its eyes and take whatever comes from the President's hand. Its confirmation of Cabinet nominees will not in the future be as perfunctory as it has been during the last half century. But the Warren incident has not, after all, given the usage its quietus. The old custom will still hold good, with the limitation that a President, in availing himself of it, must exercise caution lest he nominate any person whose career makes him especially open to attack as unsuitable for the particular post to which he is nominated.[1]

Closely linked with the power of appointment is that of removal. On this question the Fundamental Law of the Constitution is silent—an omission which has left the ground clear for violent controversies. Are the advice and consent of the Senate necessary to the removal of a Federal officer as well as to his appointment? The question came up in the House of Representatives in 1789 on the discussion of a

[1] It should scarcely be necessary to add that this account of the Warren incident must not be taken to imply any expression of opinion by the present writer as to whether the personal objections raised by the Senate to the nominee were justified. It is simply a record that the nomination was challenged on the grounds alleged.

bill for the establishment of one of the departments. In its original form the bill provided that the head of the department should be 'removable by the President.' Some members objected to this clause on the ground that the power of removal ought not to be exercised by the President, while others thought it unnecessary, holding that this power was already implicitly vested in him by the Constitution and that a recognition of the authority of the House to grant it would involve a recognition of the authority of the same body to withdraw it. Finally, a clause was substituted which implied, instead of expressly stating, that the power of removal belonged to the President.

During this debate

'four interpretations of the Constitution were given: (1) that the power of removal was to be exercised by the President alone; (2) that it was to be exercised by him only with the advice and consent of the Senate; (3) that officers could be removed only by impeachment; and (4) that the Constitution had left the question to be regulated by Congress. The first interpretation was the one held by Mr. Madison and the majority of the House.'[1]

The position then taken by both branches of Congress —for the Senate, of course, co-operated with the House in passing the bill—was thus in conflict with the opinion expressed in the *Federalist* (No. 77) by Alexander Hamilton in his attempt to quiet the fears

[1] Professor Lucy M. Salmon, *History of the Appointing Power of the President*, reprinted in 1886 from the Papers of the American Historical Association, vol. i. no. 5. Miss Salmon's treatise not only gives a full account of this debate but provides a valuable history of the whole subject up to the time of its publication.

of those who thought the Constitution gave the President too much control over appointments. ' No one,' he said, ' could fail to perceive the entire safety of the power of removal if it must thus be exercised in conjunction with the Senate.'[1]

It is worth noting that the Constitution of the Confederacy,—as a result, no doubt, of seventy years' experience of the working of the system of the United States—dealt with this matter more precisely. Its article on the appointing power of the President included the following clause:

> ' The principal officer in each of the executive departments and all persons connected with the diplomatic service may be removed from office at the pleasure of the President. All other civil officers of the executive department may be removed at any time by the President, or other appointing power, when their services are unnecessary, or for dishonesty, incapacity, inefficiency, misconduct, or neglect of duty ; and, when so removed, the removal shall be reported to the Senate, together with the reasons therefor.'

In the United States the question was by no means settled by the action of Congress in 1789, but became later the occasion of sharp conflicts between the executive and the legislature. In 1867 Congress passed a Tenure of Office Act for the purpose of preventing President Andrew Johnson from dismissing Stanton, his Secretary of War. This statute specifically gave the Senate the power of preventing

---

[1] According to Lord Acton, however, Hamilton subsequently changed his opinion on this point. See Acton's review of Bryce's American Commonwealth, reprinted in *Essays on Liberty*, p. 578.

THE TENURE OF OFFICE ACT 145

the removal of Federal officers without its consent, and limited the President's authority to the temporary suspension of an officer during a Congressional recess. It was substantially modified shortly after Johnson went out of office, but it did not entirely disappear from the statute-book until March 3, 1887. Meanwhile there had occurred frequent and serious clashes between President and Senate, the Senate objecting to certain removals made by the President and refusing to confirm his nominations to the consequent vacancies. The Collectorship of Customs at the port of New York—an office of great value, as its occupant controls several hundred subordinates—thus became a bone of contention in 1878 under Hayes and again in 1881 under Garfield. On the latter occasion the two Senators from New York State resigned their seats in protest against the President's action. Public sympathy in this instance was with the President, and the Senators, greatly to their surprise, were rejected by the legislature of their State when they presented themselves for re-election. The most notable struggle was that between President Cleveland and the Senate in 1886, when his refusal to transmit to that body the official papers bearing upon the suspension and proposed removal of a District Attorney in Alabama was followed up by an executive message, dated March 1, 1886, which dealt broadly with the right of the Senate to sit in judgment upon the President's exercise of his functions. This message, ' strong in its logic, dignified in its tone, terse, direct, and forceful in its diction,'[1] is recognized to-day as one of the most important of American constitutional documents. The practice which has since been followed is in harmony with the spirit of the decision of 1789.

Especially is the President's power of removal recognized in the case of Cabinet officers. The reason for giving him an unfettered right of dismissing them is the same as that which justifies his free choice of them in the first instance; namely, that the satisfactory working of the government will be impossible if he cannot surround himself with an 'official family' in whom he has entire confidence. There seems to be no instance, since Johnson's time, of any attempt by the Senate to prevent the removal of a Cabinet officer. But the implications of this principle are not fully realized as yet even by the Senatorial mind. The argument for the President's appointing whom he will and dismissing whom he will is equally valid for his retaining whom he will. On February 11, 1924, however, the Senate adopted, by forty-seven votes to thirty-four, a resolution asking that President Coolidge should ' immediately request ' the resignation of the Secretary of the Navy, on account of certain official acts of his relating to the Teapot Dome scandal. In vain did the spokesmen of the minority protest that such a resolution was an invasion of executive authority; that it was wholly beyond the power of the Senate to make and unmake Cabinets; that the process of impeachment was the only method by which Congress could

---

[1] H. J. Ford, *The Cleveland Era*, ed. 1919, p. 66.

UNMAKING THE CABINET   147

remove a Cabinet officer; and that the administration of the government would be unworkable if, while the President was responsible for the execution of the laws, another body was allowed to control his choice of the agents upon whom he must rely to execute the laws. The majority speakers insisted that as the Senate, by confirming his nomination in the first instance, shared the responsibility for the appointment of the Secretary, it was entitled to inform the President that the Secretary no longer possessed its confidence and therefore ought to go —an argument which evidently struck at the root of the usage, hitherto unquestioned since 1877, that the confirmation of a Cabinet officer is a mere formality. President Coolidge made no direct reply to the Senate's resolution but issued a statement in which he pointedly refused to give it any official recognition.

> ' The dismissal,' he said, ' of an officer of the government, other than by impeachment, is exclusively an executive function. I regard this as a vital principle of our government. . . . The President is responsible to the people for his conduct relative to the retention or dismissal of public officials. I assume that responsibility.'

The knot was cut a few days later by the voluntary resignation of the Secretary, and the difference of opinion between the President and the Senate as to their respective responsibilities in the matter was therefore not put to the test. But the incident suggested that, at a time of strained relations between President and Senate, the stability of the accepted usage concerning the appointment and removal of Cabinet officers might still be exposed to considerable risk. It was, indeed, an omen, which passed unheeded, of the conflict that arose in the following year over the Warren nomination.

VIII

THE POWER OF THE PURSE

' WHO pays the piper calls the tune ' is an adage that has been notably illustrated in the development of the English Constitution. The history of the government of the United States has provided further examples of the inevitable dependence of political authority upon the power of the purse.

> ' The Commons of England,' says Mr. Taft, ' won freedom and brought about a popular government through its insistence upon holding the purse-strings ; and the Congress of the United States has exactly that control over the Executive which enables it at all times to restrain the exercise of executive power by withholding the appropriations necessary to the exercise of executive power at all. . . . In other words, the Executive is always a petitioner at the door of Congress for the money necessary to carry on public affairs ; and as long as that relation exists the frequently expressed fear that the Executive is overshadowing the Legislature is merely imaginative.' [1]

The control of the national finances is definitely given to Congress by the Fundamental Law of the American Constitution. ' The Congress shall have power to lay and collect taxes, duties, imposts and excises, to pay the debts and provide for the common

---

[1] W. H. Taft, *Four Aspects of Civic Duty*, ed. 1906, p. 108.

defence and general welfare of the United States.' Congress has power also ' to borrow money on the credit of the United States.' The authority of the Senate in financial matters is limited by the provision that ' all bills for raising revenue shall originate in the House of Representatives.' ' The Senate,' however, ' may propose, or concur with, amendments as on other bills.'

It was not foreseen in America, any more than in England, what would be the indirect political effect of this power of raising and spending money. Its share in the control of the national exchequer has given the House of Representatives a quite unanticipated influence over affairs that were supposed to have been placed outside its province. Take the treaty-making power, for instance. The President, says the Fundamental Law, ' shall have power, by and with the advice and consent of the Senate, to make treaties, provided two-thirds of the Senators present concur.' The House of Representatives, evidently, was intended to have no right at all to express an opinion on such matters. But, if it is not called in to advise or ratify, it can exercise what amounts to a veto. The Fundamental Law provides that ' no money shall be drawn from the Treasury but in consequence of appropriations made by law.' Suppose, then, that a certain proposed treaty requires some kind of financial provision to bring it into operation. What can the President and Senate do if the House happens to disagree with the policy embodied in this treaty?

TREATIES AND FINANCE

The question arose as early as 1796, when the House objected to pass any bill appropriating money for the organization of the mixed commission provided for in the Jay Treaty until it had received full information of the diplomatic steps leading to its conclusion. The President, George Washington, refused to supply such information. In the end the appropriation was voted, but by only fifty-one votes to forty-eight.[1] In 1803 President Jefferson, in preparing for the acquisition of a certain portion of American territory still held by France, avoided the risk of a deadlock by seeking the judgment of the House before entering upon his negotiations and by obtaining from it beforehand an appropriation to be used at his discretion. By the treaty which was ultimately adopted a much greater extent of territory was acquired and a much higher purchase price was paid than had first been contemplated, but the deference shown by the President to the opinion of the House in the preliminary stage doubtless helped him later to secure its authorization for the larger scheme. The purchase of Alaska in 1868 raised once more the question whether the President and the Senate could of themselves negotiate and conclude a treaty involving the payment of money which could not be appropriated without the concurrence of the House of Representatives. The matter was settled by a compromise declaration. The discovery of the possibility of ' snags ' of this

---

[1] For the whole story of this controversy see S. B. Crandall, *Treaties : Their Making and Enforcement*, ed. 1916, pp. 164-82.

kind has led to the insertion, in some treaties of later date, of a stipulation that they are not to be considered as finally concluded until the legislation has been passed that is required to bring them into effect. The power of the House to ' hold up ' a treaty in this way comes to it not through usage but as an indirect result of the financial control which it shares with the Senate under the Fundamental Law. One might say, however, that usage has established the expediency, though not technically the necessity, of the House being made aware beforehand of the general drift, at any rate, of any important treaty, in process of negotiation, that would require an appropriation of money to make it operative.

No less singular and unexpected a fate has attended the exclusion of the Senate from the power of originating bills for raising revenue. The framers of the Constitution of 1787 intended the reservation of this power to the House to amount to a substantial prerogative. It was deliberately inserted as a set-off to the disproportionate legislative influence given to the smaller States by the principle of equal State representation in the Senate. The larger States, it was thought, would gain at least a partial compensation if exceptional financial authority were given to the House of Representatives, in which seats are allotted in proportion to population. In the early days of the Republic this discrimination between the powers of the two Houses affected the language employed by the President in his public utterances. In George Washington's annual allocutions to a joint

REVENUE BILLS

assembly of the two Houses all suggestions as to revenue were introduced by the specific address, 'Gentlemen of the House of Representatives,' just as in the King's Speech the financial proposals of the English Government are specifically addressed to the House of Commons.

In practice the purpose of this clause has been entirely nullified, owing to the unexpected advantage that the Senate has taken of the permission to propose amendments. The inch granted to that body by the Fundamental Law has been stretched to an ell. It will be sufficient to quote on this point the testimony of an eminent Senatorial spokesman:

> 'This unlimited power of amendment,' says Senator Lodge, 'has made the power of originating bills to raise revenue reserved to the House of comparatively little moment. In 1883 the Senate struck out all after the enacting clause of the Tariff Bill and sent over to the House their own bill, which was adopted by the House. In 1894 the Senate changed fundamentally the Tariff Bill of that year which had come from the House, and the House accepted the Bill as amended by the Senate without any alteration. In 1909 the Tariff Bill, when returned from the Senate, carried 847 amendments. These instances will show that even on Revenue Bills, which must originate in the House, the powers of the Senate have been practically unlimited.'[1]

It is not surprising that sticklers for the constitutional prerogatives of the House—corresponding to what in England we call 'House of Commons men'—protest against this behaviour as an encroachment

[1] H. C. Lodge, *The Senate of the United States*, ed. 1921, p. 8.

upon the rights of their own body. Their position is stated by S. W. M'Call when he argues that

'at the time of the framing of the Constitution there was no such thing known as amendment by complete substitution, and the fair construction of that clause, having reference to the conditions surrounding its adoption, is that, if the House should send a Bill to the Senate imposing a tax upon an article, the Senate might amend by raising or diminishing the proposed tax as it saw fit.'[1]

Mr. M'Call mentions as an especially glaring instance what happened in 1872, when the House sent to the Senate a bill relating to a tax on coffee and the Senate substituted for it, formally as no more than an amendment, a general revision of the tariff.

Lest, however, it should be supposed that the Senate habitually pushes its technical claims to the uttermost, one must balance the story just told with a picture of remarkable self-denial. While the Fundamental Law limits the functions of the Senate in the origination of bills for raising revenue, no restriction at all is placed upon its authority in any stage of the enactment of appropriation bills. But usage has brought about a modification of this freedom. Let us quote once more from Senator Lodge:

'In practice,' he says, 'the Senate, although possessing the power to originate bills appropriating money, has ceded to the House this right in the case of the great appropriation bills. The Senate still originates bills containing an appropriation of money for a single object,

[1] In an article in the *Atlantic Monthly*, October, 1903, p. 438. See also Mr. M'Call's *The Business of Congress*, ed. 1911, pp. 27 and 161.

APPROPRIATION BILLS

but on the great supply bills it is content with its right of unlimited amendment, which it always exercises without restraint.'[1]

Senator Lodge instances this practice as disproving the frequent charge that the Senate has usurped powers not granted to it by the Fundamental Law. ' In the matter of appropriations, for example, it has yielded voluntarily in giving the House the right ' —he means, of course, the exclusive right—' to originate the great supply bills.'[2]

No one can easily deny the force of such an argument. It might not require much fortitude to refrain from meddling with bills for money-raising, but to surrender one's right to a voice in the initial consideration of how the public money should be spent—such self-restraint might well kindle on a Senator's cheek the glow of conscious virtue. Dr. Von Holst, however, gives rather a different account of the matter. According to him the concession was not voluntarily made, but is the result of the defeat of the Senate in its efforts to resist the claims of the House to exclusive jurisdiction in the initiation of the principal supply bills.[3] Be that as it may, the limitation of the powers of the Senate in this respect may now be definitely regarded as part of the accepted usages of the Constitution. ' This practice,' declares Benjamin Harrison, ' has become so settled that the House would probably refuse to consider

---

[1] H. C. Lodge, *The Senate of the United States*, ed. 1921, p. 9.
[2] *Op. cit.* p. 20.
[3] Dr. Von Holst, *The Constitutional Law of the United States*, p. 132.

a general appropriation bill sent to it by the Senate.'[1]

One must speak more doubtfully of the effect of usage on another practice of great importance in relation to the enactment of appropriation bills,— the practice, in English phrase, of ' tacking.' Has Congress the right to add ' riders ' to appropriation bills in order, by means of the threat to ' hold up ' the supplies necessary for the public service, to secure the passing of measures in which it is interested? This method of coercion has been attempted at various times (a) by the Senate against the House, as when in 1849 it tacked a pro-slavery provision to an appropriation bill; (b) by the House against the Senate, as in 1855 and 1856 in the trouble over the Kansas-Nebraska Bill; and (c) by Congress as a whole against the President, who has constitutionally the right of vetoing the whole of an appropriation bill but not of vetoing any individual items in it.

The instances just mentioned under (a) and (b) are believed to have been the last attempt of either branch of the legislature to use this means of coercing the other. It has figured much more prominently in the perennial struggles between President and Congress. In 1867 Congress effectively utilized the expedient of ' tacking ' as a weapon in its conflict with Andrew Johnson. It added to an appropriation bill a clause which virtually deprived the President of the control of the military forces. Rather than interfere with the soldiers' receipt of their pay,

[1] B. Harrison, *This Country of Ours*, ed. 1898, p. 61.

Johnson signed the bill, but under protest. Encouraged by this victory, a later Congress attempted in 1879 and 1880 to employ a similar means of imposing its will upon President Hayes. In one of his veto messages he denounced this policy as involving ' a radical, dangerous, and unconstitutional change in the character of our institutions.'

' To say,' he declared, ' that a majority of either or both of the Houses of Congress may insist on the approval of a bill under the penalty of stopping all of the operations of the government, for want of the necessary supplies, is to deny to the Executive that share of the legislative power which is plainly conferred by the second section of the seventh article of the Constitution. It strikes from the Constitution the qualified negative of the President.'

It would destroy, he added, the constitutional distribution of powers among the co-ordinate branches of the government. At one stage of this controversy a special session of Congress, called for the express purpose of making appropriations that had been ' held up ' by the deadlock, closed without making any provision for the payment of marshals and deputy marshals. As the result of exhortations addressed to them by the President these officials patriotically continued for the time to discharge their duties without salary.

President Hayes persisted in vetoing the obnoxious bills, his opponents failed to obtain the majority required to pass them over his veto, and in the end Congress was compelled to separate the appropriations from the riders. In his monograph on ' The

Administration of President Hayes,' which tells the whole story of the controversy in detail, Professor J. W. Burgess declares that this victory of the President over Congress would alone have been ' sufficient to have made President Hayes' administration immortal.' ' He had vindicated the right and power of the national government to regulate by national law subjects made national by the Constitution and to enforce such national law by national officials '—this refers to the nature of the legislation proposed, which had to do with the employment of armed forces to keep the peace at elections in the Southern States—' and he had prevented the parliamentary system of government . . . from displacing the check-and-balance system provided by the Constitution.' Other authorities on American constitutional practice do not fully share Professor Burgess's conviction that the result of the Hayes controversy decided the matter for all time. Lord Bryce uses carefully guarded language on the subject.

> ' This victory,' he remarks, ' which was of course due to the fact that the dominant party in Congress could not command a two-thirds majority, was deemed to have settled the question as between the Executive and the Legislature, and may have permanently discouraged the latter from recurring to the same tactics.' [1]

Professor C. A. Beard, who in the 1915 edition of his *American Government and Politics* had said of the practice of attaching riders to appropriation bills that it ' is somewhat discredited and is seldom

---

[1] Lord Bryce, *The American Commonwealth*, ed. 1922, vol. i. p. 214.

employed,' says in the 1924 edition that it 'is somewhat discredited and is employed only in exceptional circumstances.' And Mr. Taft notes instances of its employment as late as his own administration and even President Wilson's.[1]

One may reasonably conclude that, while the Fundamental Law of the Constitution leaves Congress at perfect liberty to append riders to appropriation bills, some progress has been made toward the establishment of a constitutional usage forbidding the practice. At any rate public opinion would condemn its frequent employment. But occasions might still conceivably arise in which a Congress, strong in popular support, might feel emboldened to avail itself of this means of overcoming the resistance of a stubborn President to measures which the country wished to see on the statute-book. In such a crisis, the fact that riders are not expressly forbidden by the Fundamental Law would probably be held to justify Congress in having recourse to this unusual instrument of coercion.

[1] W. H. Taft, *Our Chief Magistrate and his Powers*, ed. 1916, p. 25.

IX

THE RESIDENT CONGRESSMAN

'A PROPHET is not without honour save in his own country and in his own house.' The American politician, however, loses all opportunity of prophesying if he lacks honour at home. For there has been established a usage which prohibits anyone from seeking to represent in Congress a ' district ' (*Anglice*, constituency) in which he does not himself reside. No such restriction is to be found in the Fundamental Law, and there is good reason to believe that an attempt to embody this custom in a statute would be pronounced ' unconstitutional ' by the Supreme Court. The best authorities hold that neither Congress nor any State Legislature has power to prescribe any additional qualifications for a Representative in Congress any more than for a President. The Fundamental Law requires that a Representative must, when elected, be an inhabitant of the State in which he is chosen, but, beyond that, it imposes no geographical limitation. Indeed, it does not even require the division of a State into Congressional districts. Strictly speaking, it regards the constituency of a Congressman as consisting of the people of the whole State. Theoretically, he represents them all, just as a Senator does. Respect

A GEOGRAPHICAL BAN

is paid to this theory in the formalities of the debates, where a member indicates another member by the name not of his district, as in Parliament, but of his State. Thus, a previous speaker will be referred to not as ' the gentleman from the Fifth District of Alabama ' or ' the gentleman from the Twenty-first District of Pennsylvania '—much less as ' the gentleman from Tuscaloosa ' or ' the gentleman from Altoona '—but as ' the gentleman from Alabama ' or ' the gentleman from Pennsylvania.'

To the rule thus imposed by usage there are only very rare exceptions. Within a single large city, like Greater New York, which sends more than twenty Representatives to the House, a resident in an up-town district may sometimes sit for a down-town district. Mr. Champ Clark, too, refers in his autobiography to a certain member who represented the Atlanta district of Georgia although he lived in another part of that State.[1] But the limitation is so generally enforced that it may be regarded as virtually an invariable feature of the American political system. It exerts upon the public life of the country an influence which few Americans adequately realize.

In the first place, it obviously excludes from Congress a large number of able men who have been unfortunate enough to make their homes in districts which already house other ambitious politicians of their own party. ' If ten statesmen live in the same street, nine will be thrown out of work,' comments Lord Acton in his review of Bryce's *American*

[1] Champ Clark, *My Quarter Century of American Politics*, vol. ii. p. 294.

Commonwealth. Few neighbourhoods, perhaps, can boast of such a superfluity of public men of the highest quality. Still it is true, as Dr. C. A. Beard remarks, that Providence has not made a geographical distribution of brains, and it may well happen that one small locality is well provided with political talent while another is destitute thereof. How this practice may obstruct the path of a man who ultimately makes his way into the House is illustrated in the career of Champ Clark, afterward leader of the Democratic party in Congress. He tells us in his autobiography that it prevented him from entering the House as early as he expected. When he went to Missouri, he ' located ' in a district where there were more Democrats in the prime of life fit to be members of Congress—all of them older than he, their ages ranging from thirty to sixty—than in any other rural Congressional district in the United States, and he had a hard fight against local competitors to secure the nomination.[1] The restriction has the further effect of excluding anyone domiciled in a district where his own party is in a perpetual minority. He is prevented from offering himself to some other constituency where his political creed would be acceptable. Goldwin Smith refers, in his *Reminiscences*, to the disability thus suffered by G. W. Curtis, to whose efforts, he says, was largely due the reform of the American Civil Service. ' Unfortunately,' he remarks, ' he lived in an electoral district where the opposite party had the majority, and thus

[1] *Op. cit.* vol. i. p. 163.

PRECARIOUS SEATS

by the fatuous localism which the Americans have imposed upon themselves he was debarred from doing his best for the country.'[1]

Moreover, when a candidate has once been elected, this restriction makes his tenure of a seat much more precarious than it would otherwise be. He knows from the first that, unless he retains the favour of his own constituency, his career in Congress is at an end. He cannot transfer his candidature to any other district unless he transfers his domicile also, like a dissatisfied husband or wife who migrates to Nevada with a view to an easier divorce. If he is unlucky enough to fall out with the local boss of his own party, he is done for. The knowledge of this sword of Damocles hanging over him stimulates many a Representative to exert himself inordinately in securing largesse for his constituency from the public purse. In England there are effective guarantees against raids upon the Exchequer for the advantage of individual constituencies. No national appropriations are made for local improvements, and the system of Cabinet responsibility for public expenditure is enforced by a standing order of the House of Commons, dating from 1713, which prohibits any motion by a private member to insert an item in an appropriation bill or to increase any item beyond the sum asked for by the government. In the Congressional system there are no such safeguards against extravagance, and Representatives take ample advantage of their freedom, realizing

[1] Goldwin Smith, *Reminiscences*, ed. 1910, p. 373.

164   THE RESIDENT CONGRESSMAN

that their chances of re-election may depend upon the spoils they bring home. Professor H. J. Ford quotes a significant advertisement, corresponding to an English election address, inserted in a local paper by a Wisconsin Congressman who was a candidate for re-election. His appeal for a renewal of confidence was based upon a record of Congressional services which included such items as these :

'He worked with Congressman Stafford and procured an appropriation of $50,000 for a new Custom House warehouse to be built on the east side. He worked with Congressman Stafford to secure the appropriation of $75,000 for a new lightship to be placed in Milwaukee Bay. He straightened out the Kinnickinnic River appropriation so that the city could go ahead with the work.'[1]

The biographer of T. B. Reed, the distinguished Republican leader and Speaker, tells us that he obtained his opportunity of entering Congress through the constituency's dissatisfaction with his predecessor's conduct in setting national above local interests.

'Mr. Burleigh, the sitting member, had weakened himself politically by a proceeding which was entirely to his honour. The Kittery Navy Yard was situated in the county in which he lived, and he had caused an investigation of alleged corruption in connection with it. By this action he had incurred the hostility of the most powerful politicians of his party in Maine.'[2]

The path of a Congressman who has made himself a power in the House is beset by another danger.

[1] H. J. Ford, *The Cost of our National Government*, ed. 1910, p. 86.
[2] S. W. M'Call, *Life of Thomas Brackett Reed*, ed. 1914, p 40.

In America a party leader whose influence on legislation makes his removal from Congress desirable in the eyes of his political opponents is exposed to the deadly weapon of the 'gerrymander.' William M'Kinley, for instance, was elected to Congress in 1876 from the Eighteenth Congressional District of Ohio. In 1890, after he had acquired national prominence through the passing of the Tariff Act which bears his name, he lost his seat. While the number of Representatives from any State is determined by Congress, the areas of the several Congressional districts within that State are delimited by the State Legislature. During M'Kinley's absence in Washington the control of the Ohio Legislature had been acquired by the Democrats. In order to prevent his re-election they rearranged the boundaries of the Eighteenth District, removing from it certain staunchly Republican counties and adding to it certain other counties that were accustomed to vote the Democratic ticket. The result was M'Kinley's defeat at the 1890 election. Fortunately for his career, his Congressional record had given him such prominence that his party adopted him as its candidate for the Governorship of Ohio in 1891, and his election to that office proved the stepping-stone to the Presidency. But the gerrymander had effectually brought his membership of Congress to an end. A similar intrigue in Illinois had driven from Congress in 1886 William Ralls Morrison, a Democratic leader, who had sat in the House for fourteen years and for three terms had been chairman of the important Committee on Ways and Means, in which capacity he had introduced several tariff measures that came within a few votes of passing. He subsequently rendered useful non-partisan service to the country as a member, and for several years the chairman, of the Interstate Commerce Commission, to which he was appointed by President Cleveland, but while he was in the prime of life—he was forty-four at the time—his political career was absolutely terminated by this expedient of the gerrymander. But for the usage which limits membership of Congress to residents within the constituency, the means taken to get rid of these distinguished politicians would have been futile, and the attempt would never have been made. However ingenious the Democrats of Ohio might have been, they could never have so carved the map of the State as to leave no chance for a Republican anywhere, and if it had been possible for Mr. M'Kinley to flee for refuge to some other constituency it would not have been worth while to employ such an extraordinary device to dislodge him from the Eighteenth District. Other prominent party leaders, like Blaine and Garfield, escaped a similar fate through the good fortune of living in constituencies which were so overwhelmingly of their own political faith that juggling with a county here and a county there could not have affected the election results. Whether a gerrymander is attempted or not, the assurance that a Congressman ousted from his home district is ousted from the House altogether, induces an exceptional concentration of party resources to compass the defeat of a member who has made himself an unusually redoubtable adversary.

In considering the results of this usage we must not confine our attention to the known instances of Congressmen who have lost their seats because they did not keep 'solid' with their constituents, or because the other side utilized against them the device of the gerrymander. We have also to take into account its effect in discouraging the candidature of men who do not think it worth while to embark on a political career unless it offers them at least a fair prospect of continuity. For one man of political ability who fails of re-election from one of these causes, there are probably ten who are deterred, by their appreciation of the risks involved, from running for Congress at all. They are not prepared to stake everything on the chance of an unbroken popularity with the voters of a single constituency. So they turn to some other career that is not exposed to these peculiar dangers.

Is it any wonder that, under these conditions, Congress is notoriously deficient in men qualified to undertake important responsibilities? In the chapter on 'The House of Representatives' in his *Congressional Government* Mr. Woodrow Wilson notes the lack in Congress, as compared with Parliament, of 'authoritative leaders' whose figures are 'very distinct and very conspicuous to the eye of the world.'

> 'Our parties,' he says, 'have titular leaders at the polls in the persons of candidates, and nominal creeds in the

resolutions of conventions, but no select few in whom to trust for guidance in general policy of legislation or to whom to look for suggestions of opinion.'

Mr. Wilson attributes this deficiency to the committee system, but it may better be explained by the constitutional usage which discourages men of ability and independence from entering Congress in the first place, so that, to quote from Dr. C. A. Beard, ' only men who are willing to devote their lives to shaking hands, slapping backs, carrying on petty trades, and wheedling appointing officers will stand for the legislature,' with the result that ' instead of statesmen capable of taking the large view of things we get shrewd men with the qualifications of the successful horse trader.' [1]

These unfortunate conditions affect the quality of the Senate as well as of the House. As Mr. Wilson remarks in his chapter on the Senate in the book quoted above :

' There cannot be a separate breed of public men reared specially for the Senate. It must be recruited from the lower branches of the representative system, of which it is only the topmost part. No stream can be purer than its sources. The Senate can have in it no better men than the best men of the House of Representatives ; and if the House of Representatives attract to itself only inferior talent, the Senate must put up with the same sort.'

Hence the complaint of Mr. Glenn Frank, the editor of the *Century Magazine*, when he laments that

as likely as not we place our foreign affairs in the hands of a Senate committee made up of small-town lawyers

[1] C. A. Beard, *American Government and Politics*, ed. 1924, p. 29.

AN ENGLISH PRECEDENT 169

who have never travelled extensively, who cannot read or speak any language other than English, who are not students of world history or world economics—men who bring to the politics of a planet the vision of a parish.'[1]

It may help us to realize the loss which the public life of America suffers from this usage if we consider how many of the most distinguished figures in the history of Parliament would have been debarred from a political career if a similar restriction had been in force in England. It is not, perhaps, generally known that at one time it was necessary for a member of the House of Commons to be a resident of the county or borough which he represented. The requirement was imposed by an act of Henry V.'s reign. It began to lapse in Tudor times, when the statute was evaded by the admission of strangers to free burghership. It was formally repealed in 1774.[2]

' It was found by experience,' remarks a great American lawyer, ' that boroughs and cities were often better represented by men of eminence and known patriotism, who were strangers to them, than by those chosen from their own vicinage. And to this very hour some of the proudest names in English history, as patriots and statesmen, have been the representatives of obscure, and, if one may so say, ignoble boroughs.'[3]

We cannot, of course, take it for granted that no M.P. who sits for a constituency in which he does not

[1] Glenn Frank, *An American Looks at his World*, ed. 1923, p. 339.

[2] See Sir W. R. Anson, *The Law and Custom of the Constitution*, ed. 1886, vol. i. p. 83, and Bishop Stubbs, *Constitutional History of England*, ed. 1878, vol. iii. p. 424.

[3] Joseph Story, *Commentaries on the Constitution of the United States*, par. 618.

reside would have succeeded in entering the House if he had become a candidate for his home borough or county. But we may justly conclude that many parliamentary careers would have been prematurely ended if a member rejected on seeking re-election had been debarred from offering his services to any other constituency. The list of notable parliamentary migrations would include many eminent names. Gladstone sat successively for Newark, Oxford University, South Lancashire, Greenwich, and Midlothian; Bright for Durham, Manchester, and Birmingham; Goschen for the City of London, Ripon, East Edinburgh, and St. George's (Hanover Square); Harcourt for Oxford City, Derby, and West Monmouth; Balfour for Hertford, East Manchester, and the City of London; Asquith for East Fife and Paisley; Morley for Newcastle and the Montrose Burghs; and Bonar Law for Blackfriars (Glasgow), Dulwich, Bootle, and Central Glasgow. What a difference it would have made to the course of English politics if Great Britain had not thrown off, centuries ago, the medieval practice which America still retains!

The arguments commonly advanced in its favour are that it assures the adequate protection of local interests in Congress, and that it makes that body more completely representative of the varied elements that compose the national life—in short, a truer 'mirror of the nation.' Each of these arguments is fallacious. As regards local interests 'a capable man residing elsewhere is quite as fit to

LAWYERS IN CONGRESS

understand and advocate such interests as a resident can be.'[1] And the fancy picture of a Congress reflecting the diversities of modern America is in glaring contrast with the reality. If there were anything in it we should find agricultural communities, for instance, largly represented by farmers. Let us turn, then, to the *Congressional Directory*, supplemented by *Who's Who in America*, to discover the occupations of the men chosen by the States in which agriculture is one of the leading industries. To the Congress in session at the time of writing Alabama has sent nine lawyers and one teacher; Arkansas, seven lawyers; Kansas, seven lawyers and one farmer; Kentucky, nine lawyers and one secretary; North Carolina, nine lawyers and one farmer; Tennessee, nine lawyers and one merchant; Texas, sixteen lawyers and two whose occupations are not mentioned; Virginia, seven lawyers and one lumberman; and so on. The House of Representatives is, indeed, a far more imperfect reflex of the national life than is the House of Commons. In the debates at St. Stephen's no subject can be raised on which there is not a group of members qualified to speak from intimate experience. At the Capitol there are no such varied resources of first-hand knowledge on which to draw. If the territorial basis of representation were superseded at Washington by the occupational, the most conspicuous immediate result would be a sensational disappearance of lawyers. In the House of Commons there

[1] Lord Bryce, *Modern Democracies*, vol. ii. p. 53.

are ninety lawyers out of a total of 615 members. But among the 435 members of the House of Representatives there are no less than 262 lawyers.[1] From the earliest days of the Republic until now lawyers have constituted a majority of each house of Congress. In connection with what has been said above as to the intellectual quality of Congress it should be noted that few of the lawyers who thus make their way into the House are men who have made any mark, or who give any promise of making their mark, in their profession. Most of them are country lawyers from small towns. I am not forgetting that Thomas Jefferson was a country lawyer, and so was Abraham Lincoln. But, as a class, in the twentieth century, country lawyers are by no means highly qualified for the task of government. In these days, much more than fifty or a hundred years ago, lawyers of ability turn to the remunerative field of ' corporation ' practice in the cities, and the lawyer who stays in his home district and runs for Congress is apt to be a man of commonplace quality and small professional prospects, to whom a political career offers greater attractions than are within his reach elsewhere.

The real reason for the perpetuation of the existing custom is the argument of the loaves and fishes. It helps to maintain the traditional system of treating the national Treasury as a source of local profit. Moreover, membership of Congress is itself a coveted financial prize. Why, then, should it be given away to an outsider ? It may be true that an income of

[1] Lindsay Rogers in the *New Republic*, July 30, 1924, p. 272.

$10,000 a year, even with the valuable perquisites that are thrown in, means nothing better than genteel poverty in Washington, but the rural aspirant for Congress does not know it. To him such a salary looks like assured comfort, not to say luxury.

'Some men in the House of Representatives,' says Mr. W. C. Redfield, ' are placed by political accidents amid affairs too vast for their comprehension. The salary paid them is larger than they can earn in private life, and is at times their reason for going to Congress. Thus said a one-term member before members' secretaries were paid directly by the House : " I'm living on my allowance for clerk hire, my wife doing my work. The $15,000 I get for two years will set me up in a little banking business when my term expires." '[1]

This conception of a seat in Congress as a *bonne bouche* leads sometimes to the adoption of a system of rotation within a constituency, so that the benefit shall be equally shared by its component sections. There is an understanding that, if county A has the nomination this year, county B shall have it at the next election, and county C at the election after that. In the instance, mentioned above, of Mr. T. B. Reed's first election to Congress, one of the difficulties in the way of his securing the nomination was the fact that he lived in a county which had already been rewarded out of its due proportion. There was a struggle in the nominating convention between the delegates from this county and those from the other county included in the district, who

[1] W. C. Redfield, *With Congress and Cabinet*, ed. 1924, p. 45. The annual salary, as this quotation suggests, was then $7,500.

contended that it was time for one of their men to have a turn.

The restriction of seats in Congress to local residents is the oldest of all the usages of the American Constitution. It antedates even the Fundamental Law itself. It is a survival of the intense localism of colonial days, which persisted in America after it had been abandoned in the mother country. (The practice is unknown, we may note in passing, in Canada or Australia, or any other part of the British Overseas Dominions.) Lord Bryce justly describes it as ' a custom old, universal, and as strong as law itself.'[1] It would be political suicide for any party to attempt to depart from this petty parochialism. For ' if any party were to break this custom, the opposition would have an excellent opportunity to appeal to local prejudice by nominating a man of local prominence against the outsider.'[2]

[1] Lord Bryce, *Modern Democracies*, vol. ii. p. 53.

[2] James T. Young, *The New American Government and its Work*, ed. 1923, p. 76.

X

MISCELLANEOUS USAGES

It is convenient to group together in a single chapter certain miscellaneous usages that require only a comparatively brief consideration.

PUBLIC SESSIONS OF CONGRESS

The Fundamental Law, while requiring each House of Congress to 'keep a journal of its proceedings and from time to time publish the same, excepting such parts as may in their judgment require secrecy,' does not impose upon either House the obligation to hold its sessions in public. To-day, however—with one important exception to be discussed presently—it would be regarded as a breach of constitutional usage for the doors of either chamber to be closed during debate.

The Continental Congress, a single-chamber body which preceded the Congress established by the Constitution of 1787, was accustomed to meet with closed doors. This secrecy was held to be necessary, for the reason that ' it was the executive as well as legislative body; names of persons and characters came perpetually before them; and much business was constantly on hand which would have been embarrassed if it had gone to the public before it was finished.'[1] The newly-created House of Representatives first met on April 1, 1789, and spent the first few days in the transaction of merely formal business. On April 8 it threw open its doors for all discussions, and since then they have never been closed during the hours of session except in rare instances of public danger.

The Senate, on the other hand, at first held all its sessions in private. This difference in the practice of the two Houses was justified on the ground that, while the House of Representatives directly represented the people, who therefore had a right to know what was being said and done in their name, the Senate, on the other hand, being at that time elected by the State Legislatures, was not immediately responsible to the general community. Attempts, however, were made at an early stage of the history of the Senate to assimilate its practice to that of the House. Resolutions in favour of throwing its proceedings open to the public were proposed and defeated year after year. An agitation to that end was also carried on in the press, notably by the *National Gazette*, the personal organ of Thomas Jefferson. The thin end of the wedge was at last inserted on February 11, 1793, when it was decided, without a division, that the question whether Albert Gallatin, who had been elected a Senator from Pennsylvania, was qualified for a seat —objection had been raised to his admission on the

[1] Jared Sparks, quoted by Max Farrand, *The Records of the Federal Convention*, vol. iii. p. 478.

OPENING THE SENATE DOORS 177

ground that he had not fulfilled the constitutional requirement of having been a citizen of the United States for nine years—should be debated with open doors. The experiment of this departure from custom convinced the most conservative that no untoward results would follow the adoption of a more generous rule, and on February 24 a resolution was passed that, from the commencement of the next session, the legislative sessions of the Senate should be open and that a gallery should be constructed for the use of strangers. Meanwhile privacy had not involved secrecy also. The question had been whether the public should be admitted to hear the debates, not whether Senators should be allowed to communicate particulars of the debates to outsiders. It is evident from contemporary writings that members of the Senate did not hesitate to reveal what had passed in that body. The exclusion of strangers during this period had one curious and unanticipated effect. It tended to lessen the prestige of the Senate as compared with the House. There was no opportunity for a Senator to gain a popular reputation by speeches which were listened to by little more than a score of colleagues and were not reported in the press. So ambitious politicians of oratorical ability preferred to be elected to the House rather than to the Senate.

On the same day that the Senate decided to hold its legislative sessions in public it further resolved that, upon the motion of any Senator seconded by another Senator, the doors should be closed for any

H.A.C.

discussion requiring secrecy. An instance of the enforcement of this rule was the discussion of the Jay Treaty in 1795. Later rules made the practice in this respect more definite. It was decided in 1800 that all confidential communications by the President to the Senate should be kept inviolably secret, and that all treaties laid before the Senate should be kept secret until the injunction of secrecy was taken off by a Senate resolution, and in 1820 that all information or remarks touching or concerning the character or qualifications of any person nominated by the President to office should be kept secret. From these two rules has resulted the practice, observed until this day, of holding all executive sessions in private; *i.e.* all sessions in which the Senate considers Presidential communications respecting nominations to office or the conclusion of treaties. These sessions are not ordinarily held on separate days from those mainly devoted to legislative business, but are intercalated in the ordinary proceedings as occasion may require. A debate may be in progress on some bill or resolution when suddenly a motion is proposed and adopted that the Senate go into executive session, and straightway the galleries are cleared, the press gallery not excepted. This custom of the Senate's sitting in secret for the transaction of executive business has had one incidental development that should be of interest to students of linguistic idiom. It has so impressed itself on the popular mind that to-day, in common parlance in America, ' going into execu-

tive session' is commonly used as a synonym for
'meeting in private.' When, for instance, in a
report of a Methodist conference or of a political or
educational convention, one reads that at a certain
stage of the proceedings the assembly 'went into
executive session,' the use of this phrase is not
intended to suggest anything as to the nature of the
business thereafter transacted. It simply means
that at this point reporters and other outsiders were
excluded.

The practice of holding the executive sessions of
the Senate with closed doors has provoked from an
eminent English writer the comment that ' it is one
of the most remarkable characteristics of the American
democracy how much of its working is withdrawn
from the public eye.'[1] When one considers the
delicate nature of much of the business transacted
on these occasions—the confirmation of the President's nominations to office, for example—it would
seem as reasonable to object to the exclusion of
reporters from an English Cabinet meeting. And,
after all, the secrecy is by no means as secret as it
looks. It is theoretically safeguarded by the threat
of severe penalties for the breach of it. By a rule
passed in 1868 any Senator, or officer of the Senate,
who discloses the secret or confidential business or
proceedings of the Senate is liable, if a Senator, to
suffer expulsion from that body, or, if an officer,
to dismissal from the service of the Senate and to
punishment for contempt. Yet, somehow or other,

[1] W. E. H. Lecky, *Democracy and Liberty*, ed. 1900, vol. i. p. 444.

when anything of special importance or interest happens in executive session the papers are able to publish pretty full reports of it the next morning. There is reason to believe that, on the whole, these reports are fairly accurate, though, as a journalist of long experience in the press gallery has pointed out, there must always be some doubt attached to the reliability of information ' which must pass through two or more persons and is based merely on the memory of what is said and done.' The same writer gives an amusing and pathetic example of the impossibility of correcting any misstatement that has once got into print.

> ' In the last session of the Senate,' he says, ' in executive session concerning the San Domingo Treaty, Senator Morgan made a vigorous protest against the newspapers putting words into his mouth that he had never spoken, pointing out that he was helpless to refute these stories, for the reason that if he should make a statement of facts he would be violating the rules of the Senate enjoining secrecy.'[1]

Every attempt to discover the source of these leakages has hitherto been unsuccessful.

> ' About ten years ago the Steering Committee of the Senate took up the idea that Mr. James Rankin Young, the executive clerk of the Senate, was guilty of giving away the secrets, and he was promptly dismissed from his position. Very few at the time believed that Mr. Young had any hand or voice in such betrayal, for he was of fine family and a high-minded and honourable gentleman. The proof of his innocence was clearly established after

[1] O. O. Stealey, *Twenty Years in the Press Gallery*, ed. 1906, p. 7.

MYSTERIOUS LEAKAGES

the next executive session by a more full and accurate report of its proceedings than usual being published the following morning, and the leak has since continued. In the meantime Mr. Young was voted into Congress by his friends in vindication of his character and conduct and in retaliation for the stigma the Senate had placed upon him.'[1]

In one conspicuous instance the Senate has departed from the otherwise invariable practice of holding its executive sessions in private. Its debates on the Versailles Treaty were carried on in public. The decision to suspend the normal rule was a shrewd move on the part of the opponents of the treaty, who calculated that the publication of the proceedings would assist their appeal to the American people against President Wilson's policy. There was also a minor exception to the usual custom in March, 1925, when it was decided by a majority vote to discuss in open session the nomination of Mr. Warren to the Attorney-Generalship. It would be rash to express any opinion as to the prospect of the ultimate rescinding of the present prohibitory rule. If it has retained its place in the code of Senatorial procedure it is not for the lack of frequent endeavours to get rid of it.[2] Should the practice of the Senate in this respect ever be changed, it will probably be from the conviction that the national

---
[1] *Op. cit. ib.*
[2] A speech made by Senator Orville H. Platt, of Connecticut, in support of one of these attempts was a carefully prepared review of the history of the subject, and has been largely drawn upon for information used in the writing of this chapter. It is reported in the *Congressional Record* of April 13, 1886.

interest would be better served by a policy of open debates than by an ostensible exclusiveness which cannot actually be maintained. At any rate, the usage which requires all the proceedings of both Houses, with this single exception, to be accessible both to representatives of the press and to the general public may be regarded as firmly established in the American constitutional system. An attempt to break it down would have to challenge an overwhelming consensus of popular opinion in its support.

THE COMBINATION OF FEDERAL AND STATE OFFICE

The Fundamental Law makes the holding of any Federal office a bar to membership of either House of Congress. This limitation is, of course, essential to the attempted separation of legislative and executive functions. Usage prohibits further the combination of membership of Congress or the holding of a Federal office with either membership of a State Legislature or the holding of a State office. In most instances these restrictions might be adequately explained by the impossibility of being in two places at the same time. It is physically out of the question for anyone to discharge simultaneously the duties of a Representative at Washington and an Assemblyman or State official at Albany. Sometimes, however, no geographical difficulty would arise, any more than in the case of an M.P. who was also Lord Mayor of London. There are Federal offices at every State capital. But in any case no

A GEOGRAPHICAL BALANCE 183

such combination as those mentioned above is ever attempted, partly owing to the general American dislike of anything that savours of pluralism, and partly, perhaps, from a feeling that it is well to avoid any risk of confusion between the claims of the Union and of the State upon the public service of the individual citizen.

THE GEOGRAPHICAL DISTRIBUTION OF OFFICES

In his farewell address George Washington uttered a warning against what has since come to be known in America as ' sectionalism.' Recognizing that the North and the South, the East and the West, had each of them distinct commercial and industrial interests, he pointed out that these special interests depended for their preservation upon a patriotic spirit which subordinated the part to the whole.

As regards the legislative branch of the government, the Fundamental Law of the Constitution saw to it that no section of the country should have any just cause for complaining that it lacked opportunity of making its influence felt in national affairs. To the Senate every State, large or small, sends two members, while in the House representation is based on population.

No provision was made for ensuring that an equally catholic principle should prevail in the executive and judicial branches. There is nothing in the Fundamental Law to prevent the whole membership of the Cabinet and of the Supreme Court from being drawn from one section of the country¹ or even from a single State. But constitutional usage has come to require that the personnel of these bodies shall, as far as possible, be representative of the whole country. The appointment of several members from the same State or of a preponderance of members from New England, let us say, would be regarded as a departure from a wholesome practice. There is no attempt to keep anything like an exact balance. A Democratic President may naturally be expected to show favour toward the South, while a Republican may lean toward the States which are the strongholds of his own party. There may be reasons too, from time to time, arising from the individual quality of the available choices, why one section of the country should be allotted more than its mathematical proportion. But the political memoirs show that a new President, in constructing his Cabinet, is careful to give weight to the geographical factor in making his selections, and this principle usually helps to determine the filling of a vacancy in the Supreme Court also. President Wilson drew two members of his original Cabinet from New York, and one each from New Jersey (his own State), Pennsylvania, North Carolina, Tennessee, Texas, Missouri, Nebraska, and California. President Harding, who was from Ohio, selected two from Pennsylvania and one each from Massachusetts, New York, Ohio,

[1] The official statistics of population group the States in nine divisions—New England, Middle Atlantic, East North Central, West North Central, South Atlantic, East South Central, West South Central, Mountain, and Pacific.

JUDICIAL INDEPENDENCE 185

Indiana, Iowa, Michigan, New Mexico, and California. At the beginning of 1925 the Supreme Court was composed of a Chief Justice from Connecticut, and Associate Justices from Massachusetts (two), Tennessee (two), Minnesota, Utah, Wyoming, and California.

THE INTEGRITY OF THE SUPREME COURT

There is no other element of the American system of government that enjoys such independence as the Federal judiciary. The President holds office for four years, Senators for six, and Representatives for two, and in each case a renewal of office can be obtained only by the process of re-election. In most of the States not only the Governor and the members of the State Legislature but the judges also are similarly elected by a popular vote for a term of years. The Federal judges, on the other hand, whether of the Supreme or of any other Court, hold their seats during good behaviour, and are removable only by impeachment. It is provided, moreover, by the Fundamental Law of the Constitution, that their salaries shall not be diminished during their continuance in office.

In the case of the Supreme Court of the United States this establishment of the judges in an impregnable position above the chances and changes of electoral contests has important political consequences. For their authority to interpret the Fundamental Law gives them the power of life and death over every Congressional statute. If they pronounce it 'unconstitutional' it becomes *ipso facto* invalid. Many legislative proposals have been safely piloted through the shoals and storms of the two Houses only to be shattered upon this rock.

In the working of such a system there are bound to be occasions when the invalidating of a new Act of Congress by a Supreme Court judgment causes widespread disappointment. It is impossible to learn in advance what the decision of the Court will be on the constitutionality of any bill introduced into Congress. Not until it has passed through all its stages and is actually being put into operation can there be presented the test case which alone can become the subject of the Court's consideration. If the decision is unfavourable, the advocates of the measure usually see whether they can re-draft it in such a way as to eliminate the features which the Court has held to be in conflict with the Fundamental Law. Sometimes this is possible, and the revised statute may come successfully through the ordeal, but more often the inconsistency is so radical that the second attempt leads only to a second failure. If the measure thus blocked is powerfully supported by public opinion its fate is likely to provoke not only disappointment but resentment, and people begin to ask whether there is no way of over-riding the decision of the tribunal which has thus thwarted a popular demand.

There is, conceivably, such a way. The section of the Fundamental Law which creates the Supreme Court does not specify the number of judges of which it shall be composed. The decision of that matter is, inferentially, left to Congress. This omission obviously gives an opportunity for a party that controls both the Executive and the Legislature to tune the Court in its favour. Suppose that an interpretation of the Fundamental Law by the Court quashes a Congressional enactment which has been carried in both Houses by an overwhelming vote and is approved by the President. If President and Congress were agreed, it would be easy enough first to pass an Act enlarging the bench,[1] and then to appoint a sufficient number of new judges, of the right political colour, to reverse the unpopular decision and make the will of Congress supreme. Such a solution of the difficulty might be compared to the exercise of the royal prerogative of the creation of new peers to bring to an end a deadlock between Lords and Commons, or to the power given to the Government of the Dominion of Canada to add six members to the Senate in cases of serious disagreement between the two Houses. What is there to prevent a *coup d'état* of this kind ? Nothing whatever in the text of the Fundamental Law.

The expedient of increasing and then ' packing ' the Court has, in fact, sometimes been employed.

' The Federalists,' says Dr. Westel W. Willoughby, ' in 1801 changed the number of Federal judges for political reasons. In 1866 Congress reduced the number of Supreme Court justices from ten to seven in order to

[1] The Supreme Court consists at present of a Chief Justice and eight Associate Justices.

deprive President Johnson of the opportunity of making appointments. After all fear of Johnson's reconstruction policy was over the Act of 1869 was passed, by which the number of justices was raised to nine. The influence the appointment of the two new justices under this last Act had upon the legal tender decisions gave rise to the suspicion that the two new justices, Strong and Bradley, received their appointments because of their known or suspected opinions regarding the constitutionality of a legal tender issue.'[1]

Of the same incident the following account is given by Woodrow Wilson in the introductory chapter of his *Congressional Government* :

' In December, 1869, the Supreme Court decided against the constitutionality of Congress's pet Legal Tender Acts ; and in the following March a vacancy on the bench opportunely occurring, and a new justiceship having been created to meet the emergency, the Senate gave the President to understand that no nominee unfavourable to the debated Acts would be confirmed, two justices of the predominant party's way of thinking were appointed, the hostile majority of the Court was outvoted, and the obnoxious decision reversed.'

Since then there have been several occasions when there has been an equally strong temptation to have recourse to this desperate method of over-riding a Supreme Court decision. But it has always been resisted, partly from a feeling that it would not be ' playing the game,' and partly from the conviction that such a policy would in the long run inflict upon

[1] W. W. Willoughby, *The Supreme Court of the United States*, ed. 1890, p. 103.

THE INTEGRITY OF THE COURT 189

the country a graver loss than would be suffered through the failure of any particular legislative proposal to become law. This sense of its danger is expressed by Benjamin Harrison when he says :

' If political interests are involved in a decision, and the decision is adverse to the party in power, the suggestion that a reversal may be secured by increasing the number of justices is very tempting to partisans, but its frequent use will be destructive, fatally so, to our constitutional union.' [1]

' We do not think of such a violation of the spirit of the Constitution as possible,' remarks Woodrow Wilson, ' simply because we share and contribute to that public opinion which makes such outrages upon constitutional morality impossible by standing ready to curse them.' [2]

It may therefore be concluded that the integrity and inviolability of the Supreme Court are secured by public opinion against the danger that any party or group, however powerful, will hereafter take advantage of the loophole offered by the letter of the Fundamental Law. No doubt there will be instances in the future, as there have been in the past, of the political complexion of possible appointees being taken into account in the filling of a vacancy in the Court when it happens to occur. But there will be no attempt to ' dilute ' the Court itself by appointing additional members for the purpose of securing the triumph of a specific policy. That is to say, there has been established a constitutional

[1] B. Harrison, *This Country of Ours*, ed. 1897, p. 314.
[2] W. Wilson, *An Old Master and other Political Essays*, ed. 1893, p. 154.

usage strong enough to prohibit the most powerful President and Congress, whatever the provocation, from taking a course which would make the Supreme Court the plaything of party politics. If the authority of the Court to interpret the Fundamental Law is in any way diminished it will not be by resort to any sharp practices but by means of a formal Constitutional Amendment which will specifically limit that authority. There is a movement, for instance, for the adoption of a Constitutional Amendment which will prevent the Court from invalidating an Act of Congress by the decision of a bare majority.

TITLES OF HONOUR

' No title of nobility shall be granted by the United States.' ' No State shall grant any title of nobility.' So runs the Fundamental Law. Madison, in No. 38 of the *Federalist*, refers to the ' absolute prohibition of titles of nobility, both under the Federal and State government,' as one of the ' most decisive ' proofs of the ' republican complexion ' of the new political system. It will be noted, however, that this prohibition does not extend to any titles of honour other than titles of nobility. There is nothing in it, for instance, to prevent the institution of a baronetage or an order of knighthood. This omission has been supplied by usage. It is neither the Fundamental Law nor any statute but a consensus of public opinion that leaves the United States without any official ' fountain of honour.' Everyone knows that fear of popular sentiment would effectually deter a President or Congress, a Governor or State Legislature, that desired to institute any definite system of rewarding public service by the conferment of such distinctions. The usage of the American Constitution as definitely forbids the creation of baronets or knights as its Fundamental Law forbids the creation of dukes or earls.

When one is told that this embargo is due to a spirit of democratic equality which objects to any suggestion that one man is better than another, one can only receive the information with a smile. Most Americans, no doubt, honestly imagine that this is so, but their own practice shows that they are mistaken. Human nature in America is very much like human nature elsewhere, and the American citizen has as eager a craving for decorations as the man of any other nationality. The only difference is that, in the United States, these decorations cannot be officially bestowed. They must not be authenticated by any Heralds' College. 'It is a very curious fact,' remarks Oliver Wendell Holmes, ' that, with all our boasted " free and equal " superiority over the communities of the Old World, our people have the most enormous appetites for Old World titles of distinction.'[1] He instances the Knights of Labour, the Knights and Ladies of Honour, the Royal Conclave of Knights and Ladies, etc. A modern list of American fraternal orders would include such organizations also as the Knights

[1] O. W. Holmes, *Over the Teacups*, ed. 1892, p. 222.

of Pythias, the Knights of Columbus, the Knights of the Golden Eagle, the Nobles of the Mystic Shrine, and the Colonial Dames.

It may be said, of course, that when Americans call themselves and one another Knights they do not use the title to imply any personal distinction. It is merely a gorgeous label for the members of a friendly society, which does not regard itself as equivalent in any degree to an Order of Merit. But this disclaimer will not apply to the use of the prefix ' Honourable,' which, according to one of the best American dictionaries,

> ' is commonly given to persons who hold or have held any considerable office under the national or State government, particularly to members and ex-members of Congress and of State legislatures, to judges, justices, and some other judicial officers, as well as to certain executive officers.'

In the two Houses of Congress alone there are at any one time over 500 members, and the total membership of the forty-eight State legislatures exceeds 7,000. One may therefore conclude that this title is probably worn by a larger number of persons in the United States than in the United Kingdom.

Moreover, in the United States one's inability to secure a handle to one's name in the manner familiar in older countries is compensated for, to a large degree, by the use of the names of offices for that purpose. When I was new to America, and had not yet become acquainted with this national peculiarity,

OFFICIAL TITLES

I noticed an occasional mention in the newspapers of a Secretary of the Interior Bliss. I wondered what particular brand of felicity an interior bliss might be, why it should be dignified by capital initials, and what necessity it could have for the services of a secretary. Presently I discovered that the allusion was to a Cabinet minister named Bliss, who held the office of Secretary of the Interior. For the sake of convenience in manipulation these handles to an official's name are sometimes abbreviated, by no means to the disadvantage of his apparent status. Thus you may find that a General So-and-so owes his title to the fact that he is a Receiver-General, or a Judge-Advocate-General, or an Assistant-Postmaster General. One of the most frequent of such adornments is 'President,' which prefaces the name not only of the occupant of the White House but of the heads of innumerable colleges, banks, railway companies, and business organizations, large and small, important and unimportant.

The number of persons thus distinguished above their fellows is immensely increased by the custom, noted in the dictionary definition quoted above, of retaining a title after the occasion for it has disappeared. All over the United States there are men who still wear the title of some office which they held ten or twenty years ago. When the historian Freeman visited America in 1882 he was sometimes embarrassed by this peculiarity.

'More than once,' he tells us, ' when I had been introduced to " Governor A," and had put myself into a proper mood of respect towards the chief magistrate of the State, I found that all that was meant was that the gentleman to whom I was speaking had been Governor in time past.'[1] The scent of the roses clings to them still.

The usage, then, which prohibits the granting of titles by any official 'fountain of honour' does not prevent the use of all manner of titles by thousands of American citizens. But has it any political effect, direct or indirect? It has at least one curious and inconvenient result. From time to time the question inevitably arises : What shall be done unto the man whom the sovereign people delighteth to honour? An individual American may have performed some conspicuous service to his own country or to humanity which obviously deserves national recognition. But, owing to the embargo upon the conferment of titles, there is no appropriate method of recognition available. When Peary discovered the North Pole everybody felt that the United States ought in some way to show its appreciation of what he had done. If the explorer had been an Englishman he would have received some distinction from the Crown, which, no doubt, would not have augmented his fame but would at least have been an expression of the admiration felt for him by his fellow-countrymen. But the American government could find no way of rewarding Peary except by making him a Rear-Admiral. Some objection was reasonably raised on the ground that his achievements were not naval, and that a rise in naval rank was not a suitable method

---

[1] E. A. Freeman, *Some Impressions of the United States*, p. 208.

of recognizing them. There have been other instances in which an American has deserved well of the nation by services of such a kind that in England they would naturally be rewarded by a Privy Councillorship or a baronetcy, or at least a knighthood. But in the United States the irresistible popular demand that he should be publicly honoured in some way could be gratified only by his appointment or election to some public office, for which he might happen to be quite unfitted. He has undertaken the task imposed upon him, and his career in office has not enhanced his reputation.

XI
CHANGES IN CONSTITUTIONAL USAGE

WHILE the content of the Law of the Constitution —whether Fundamental Law, Statute Law, or Common Law—can be exactly determined, there can obviously be no equally precise statement of its usages. In the nature of the case there can be no authority, judicial or otherwise, qualified to make an *ex cathedra* pronouncement on what is, and is not, to be regarded as coming under this category. What Dr. A. L. Lowell, the President of Harvard, has said of the usages of the English Constitution, in the introduction to his book on *The Government of England*, applies no less to those of the American Constitution also :

> ' It is impossible to make a precise list of the conventions of the Constitution, for they are constantly changing by a natural process of growth and decay, and while some of them are universally accepted, others are in a state of uncertainty.'

The present writer has had an inconvenient reminder of the risk that current events may modify the binding force of a usage that has long been accepted without question. His chapter on ' Appointment and Removal ' had been completed and was ready to go to the printer when the rejection by the Senate of the nomination of Mr. Warren as Attorney-General compelled the rewriting of the whole of that section of the chapter which relates to the confirmation of Cabinet appointments.

Some treatises on American government include in the so-called ' unwritten Constitution ' certain well-established practices which the present writer has ignored because they do not seem to him clearly entitled to be counted among constitutional usages. There is, for instance, the organization of the standing committees of Congress. The growth of the committee method of legislation, never anticipated by the founders of the Republic, is without doubt one of the most important developments of the American political system. It has had far-reaching effects on the course of events. But, after all, this method is nothing more than a particular form of parliamentary procedure—a matter of the internal arrangements of the legislative body itself. It has nothing to do with the powers of Congress or with its relation to the other branches of the government or to the nation at large, and accordingly it can no more claim a place among the usages of the Constitution than any scheme for the distribution of duties among the Judges of the Supreme Court or the executive staff at the White House. The same remark applies to the development of the Speakership of the House of Representatives into an office of party leadership instead of a neutral chairmanship as in the House of Commons.

These things are distinctive features of the American system of government, but they do not appropriately demand attention in a survey of the usages of the American Constitution.

The usages considered in this book are those which are actually in force at the time of writing. Just as a new statute may be enacted or an old one repealed, so the body of usage may be enlarged or diminished. A discussion of the subject twenty years ago would have had to take into account two usages, at least, which have since then disappeared from the list. According to the Fundamental Law, the President ' shall from time to time give to the Congress information of the state of the Union and recommend to their consideration such measures as he shall judge necessary and expedient.' George Washington and his immediate successor, John Adams, communicated their ' messages ' to Congress by word of mouth.

> ' But Jefferson,' to quote from the early editions of Bryce's *American Commonwealth*, ' when his turn came in 1801, whether from republican simplicity, or because he was a poor speaker, as his critics said, began the practice of sending communications in writing ; and this has been followed ever since.'

As late as the publication of the 1910 edition of the work quoted this was a correct statement of the invariable practice, and no one at that time would have questioned the inclusion, among constitutional usages, of the requirement that all presidential messages to Congress should be communicated in writing and should be read to that body not by the President himself but by one of its own officials. The usual spectacle on the occasion of the reception of such a message—a clerk droning out a long address to a listless assembly in a half-empty chamber—was not one that would impress a stranger with the dignity of either President or Congress. But although the tradition had come to be generally recognized as an unfortunate one, it did not occur to any President, until Mr. Wilson took office, that he had the power to break away from it. In one of his treatises on the American political system Mr. Wilson himself had described ' the fashion of written messages ' as ' firmly established,'[1] and up to the time of his own election to the Presidency he had not departed from that opinion. The idea of reverting to the original practice came to him, we are told, from a suggestion offered him by a newspaper reporter, Mr. Oliver P. Newman, in an interview shortly before he actually entered upon his office.[2] On April 8, 1913, a century-old usage of the American Constitution vanished into limbo when President Wilson appeared at the Capitol and read his first message to a joint assembly of both Houses. A tactful introduction happily disposed of any prejudice that might have arisen in the minds of conservatives who were reluctant to see any departure from the beaten paths.

[1] W. Wilson, *The State*, ed. 1904, p. 546.
[2] See David Lawrence, *The True Story of Woodrow Wilson*, ed. 1924, p. 82.

'I am very glad indeed,' said Mr. Wilson, 'to have this opportunity to address the two Houses directly and to verify for myself the impression that the President of the United States is a person, not a mere department of the government hailing Congress from some isolated island of jealous power, sending messages, not speaking naturally and with his own voice—that he is a human being trying to co-operate with other human beings in a common service. After this pleasant experience I shall feel quite normal in all our dealings with one another.'

The change was, of course, brought about the more easily because it was not, strictly speaking, an innovation but a reversion to an early custom sanctioned by the example of George Washington himself. It won general approval from both parties alike. The comment made on it by Mr. Wilson's predecessor is especially interesting :

'I think the change is a good one,' he remarks. 'Oral addresses fix the attention of the country on Congress more than written communications, and by fixing the attention of the country on Congress they fix the attention of Congress on the recommendations of the President. I cannot refrain from a smile, however, when I think of the Democratic oratory which was lost because Mr. Roosevelt or I did not inaugurate such a change. The eloquent sentences that would have resounded from the lips of Senator Ollie James or Senator John Sharp Williams, those faithful followers of Jefferson, in denunciation of " such a royal ceremony in a speech from the Throne " I could supply with little effort of the imagination. Surely a member of the Jeffersonian party has some advantage in the presidential chair.'[1]

[1] W. H. Taft, *Our Chief Magistrate and his Powers*, ed. 1916, p. 40.

The precedent set by President Wilson has since been followed by his successors, Presidents Harding and Coolidge. It does not mean the setting up of a new usage that presidential communications to Congress shall always be delivered orally. The less important ones—there are scores of them in a single year—are still transmitted in writing and read by clerks, and one of Mr. Coolidge's annual messages has reached Congress by this medium. What has happened has been simply the disappearance of the usage which for more than a hundred years forbade the President to make such communications in person.

Another change is also due to the initiative of Mr. Wilson. Reference has already been made, in the chapter on 'Accidental' Presidents, to the general understanding that it was unconstitutional for a President to leave the territory of the United States during his term of office. This limitation appears to date back to a very early period. In a speech given in the Senate on December 3, 1918, Senator Knox showed that George Washington considered himself bound by it. Shortly before the State of Rhode Island had ratified the Fundamental Law, the first President made a coaching trip to New England. He carefully and avowedly avoided going into Rhode Island because it was foreign territory to the new Union. Shortly afterwards Rhode Island accepted the Fundamental Law, and then President Washington emphasized the difference by making a special trip to that State. In the same speech Senator Knox referred to various occasions on which a President of the United States, visiting the Mexican boundary and wishing officially to meet the President of the Mexican Republic, either remained on the United States side of the bridge which connects El Paso with Juarez or advanced no further than the middle of the bridge. The usage, it is true, was not pedantically interpreted. President Cleveland, for instance, once went on a fishing trip beyond the three-mile limit in the Atlantic.[1] But it was distinctly understood to prohibit anything like a sojourn, for however brief a space of time, in foreign territory. Mr. Taft, before his election, was accustomed to spend part of his annual vacation in Canada, but as soon as he became President his choice of summer resorts was limited to American soil.

The restrictive usage was still in full vigour during the first term of the very President who in his second term broke it down. At the beginning of 1914 there was projected a great peace celebration, both in the United States and in England, of the one hundredth anniversary of the Treaty of Ghent. Mr. Walter H. Page, the United States Ambassador to Great Britain, had a plan for a partnership between the two countries, and, as a first step in its development, pressed the American President to come over to England and accept in person the gift of Sulgrave Manor, the old home of the Washingtons. He wanted ' to have the President of the United States

[1] F. J. Haskin, *The American Government*, ed. 1912, p. 5.

and the King of England stand up side by side and let the world take a good look at them.' It was only with great reluctance that Mr. Wilson, who was much attracted by the idea, felt constrained to refuse. ' The case,' he wrote, ' against the President's leaving the country, particularly now that he is expected to exercise a constant leadership in all parts of the business of the government, is very strong, and I am afraid overwhelming.'[1] Before five years had elapsed Mr. Wilson's visit to Paris brought the traditional limitation of the President's movements to an end.

In the introduction to his book on the English Constitution Professor Dicey notes that in England several practices which could once be numbered among constitutional understandings or conventions have since been converted into laws. There seems to be nothing quite analogous to this in the development of the American Constitution. But in one instance a practice which had travelled a long way on the road to becoming an established usage has been incorporated in the Fundamental Law. According to the latter document, as it existed up to 1913, the Senate of the United States was to be composed of two Senators from each State, ' chosen by the legislature thereof.' There grew up, however, in various parts of the country, a strong demand for the election of these Senators by popular vote. During the period when the method of formal amendment of the Fundamental Law was virtually given up as impracticable, the rank and file of the

[1] Burton J. Hendrick, *Life and Letters of Walter H. Page*, ed. 1922, vol. i. p. 276.

two leading parties in some of the States gained their end by a circuitous route. In their 'primaries' and other party meetings they directly expressed their choice as to any Senatorial seats that might be vacant, and the representatives whom they sent to the State Legislature went there under instructions to support the candidate whom the majority vote of the party —or its bosses—had already selected. This practice made rapid headway, and after a time the Legislatures of several of the States had as completely lost their independent discretion in the choice of a Senator as the Presidential Electors in the choice of a President. That is to say, it was becoming a part of the usage of the Constitution that the election of Federal Senators should not be made, as originally intended, by bodies presumably better fitted than the average citizen to exercise an intelligent choice, but by popular vote. The practice had one serious disadvantage from which the usage relating to Presidential Electors is free. A Presidential Elector has one duty only. As soon as he has cast his ballot for a President, his work is over. But the member of a State Legislature has many responsibilities, and the custom of choosing him with a view to the vote he will give on a single occasion and on a single issue tended to the loss of popular control over his action on matters which, theoretically, were his chief concern. The result has thus been described by Dr. A. T. Hadley :

'In the old days,' he says, ' it was never possible to elect a Legislature on the basis of State issues in a year when

ELECTION OF SENATORS

a United States Senator was going to be chosen. You might approve the position of the Republican party in your State on canals, or on prohibition, or on economical management of the State Treasury, or any one of a dozen local issues. But if you wanted to see a Democrat elected to the United States Senate, you had to vote for a Democratic candidate for the State Legislature, even if he was bibulous, extravagant, unprogressive, and averse to building the canals you wanted. His chief business, after all, was to elect a United States Senator. A Legislature has to elect a Senator twice in six years. In those States, therefore, which elected their Legislatures for two years at a time, two out of every three Legislatures were chosen on national issues and only one of the three on local ones. This gave the leaders in party politics a stronger hold over nominations and elections to the State Legislature than they would otherwise have possessed, and had an effect on the conduct of State politics and State business far more serious than has generally been recognized.'[1]

When, however, it became clear, from the progress being made toward the ratification of the Income-tax Amendment, that the modification of the Fundamental Law itself was much more practicable than had been commonly supposed, a stimulus was given to the project of securing the popular election of Senators by the prescribed process of constitutional amendment. Accordingly in 1913 this change was made, an Amendment being adopted which requires the Senators from each State to be elected ' by the people thereof '—a reversion to a plan which was considered and rejected by the Convention of 1787.

[1] A. T. Hadley, *Undercurrents in American Politics*, ed. 1915, p. 132.

On the probability of future changes in the body of usages of the American Constitution, whether by the desuetude of some now in existence or the establishment of new ones, it would be idle to speculate. The emergencies that will compel further alterations of the present American system of government lie beyond the ability of anyone to predict. But it seems reasonable to suppose that the recent revival of the method of constitutional change by formal amendment of the Fundamental Law may diminish the tendency, by lessening the need, to resort to extra-legal means of modifying or supplementing it. As to the question of the permanence of existing usages, we must beware of attaching too great importance to the mere cumulative effect of their repeated observance. They are precedents, but it is not *qua* precedents that they have their authority. Their validity depends entirely upon their usefulness at the moment. If, for instance, the Presidential Electors meeting in January, 1925, made no attempt at exercising their own discretion in the choice of a President, it was not simply because of respect for a tradition established by the action of previous Presidential Electors at quadrennial intervals up to 1921, but because the American people to-day insist on such a surrender of independence. It is not in the domain of usage but in that of the common law that precedent really exercises its influence.

The period of time during which an extra-legal practice has been observed affords no criterion as to

TESTS OF PERMANENCE 207

whether or not it has become permanently established. By the lapse of years it may have acquired the status of an accepted usage, but not of a usage that is beyond all risk of modification or even supersession. If, in 1913, one had applied the time-test to the usages then in force, one would have attributed greater validity to the custom of a President's non-appearance in Congress to communicate his message than to the forfeiture of their independence by the Presidential Electors, for the former practice had originated at an earlier date than the latter. But it disappeared suddenly, almost at a touch. After all, the determining factor seems to be public opinion. If the questions involved do not arouse general interest, a new usage may easily be established or an old one easily abrogated. On the whole, the American public is indifferent to controversies about official prerogative. It is only the professional politician, not 'the man in the street,' that troubles himself much whether the confirmation of Presidential nominations to Cabinet office shall depend on a scrutiny of the qualifications of the nominee or shall be a mere formality. The only matter that really concerns him is that the appointments, by whomsoever made, shall be good ones. The method of electing a President, however, is quite another affair. Here, the usage that the Electors shall be appointed by popular vote and shall do no more than register a preference already expressed at the polls is based on an insistent demand that, whatever machinery may be employed, the Chief Executive shall actually be the choice of the people. The only expression of a minority opinion that the present writer has discovered is to be found in the biography of Joseph Pulitzer, of the *New York World*, who is there shown to have been in favour of carrying out the provisions of the Fundamental Law in the spirit as well as in the letter. In outlining an editorial article to be written by a member of his staff in 1907, Mr. Pulitzer urged that the President ' certainly should not be nominated in the way we do nominate by machine methods and in howling conventions, but on the contrary be elected by Electors specially chosen for their superior coolness and eminence.' These Electors should be ' actually forbidden to meet together ' and should be ' compelled, as intended, to vote in forty-six separate departments segregated at the time, with the understanding that they could not know what the other States would do.'[1] If the article written was on the lines suggested, it must surely have deserved a place in an exhibition of newspaper curios. For the demand for a popular election is virtually unanimous. It is therefore inconceivable that, in any circumstances, the existing usage could break down. The only thing that could cause its disappearance would be the substitution, by an amendment to the Fundamental Law, of a method of direct election for the present indirect method. One cannot imagine a popular uprising in defence of the President's control of Cabinet appointments, but there would certainly be a revolutionary movement, if

[1] D. C. Seitz, *Joseph Pulitzer : His Life and Letters*, ed. 1924, p. 324.

necessary, to prevent the Presidential Electors from regaining their control of the election. The strength of any usage, in short, depends upon an overwhelming popular sentiment in its favour.

Are there any guiding principles or determinative forces that one can trace in the formation of the body of custom that to-day supplements or modifies the law of the Constitution? It is clear, from the account given in previous chapters, that the usage of the Constitution has been shaped, piecemeal, by the needs of the moment. It has come into existence by a process of gradual development, determined by actual emergencies that required some extra-legal means of meeting them. One may nevertheless trace in its construction the working of certain general principles which give it a consistency scarcely inferior to that of a document deliberately fashioned at one time.

In the first place, it recognizes the necessity of mutual concessions for the avoidance of a deadlock in the government. For instance, in certain matters of the highest importance, the Fundamental Law made the President and the Senate partners without precisely defining their several powers or taking any precautions to insure the possibility of their co-operation. The article which authorizes the President to do certain things ' by and with the advice and consent of ' a body with which he might, or might not, happen to be in political agreement leaves the responsibility for action indeterminate where it would have been desirable that it should be fixed.

It is often convenient for partners in a business to make a friendly arrangement among themselves for the delimitation of the powers and functions of the individual members of the firm so that there shall be no conflict or overlapping of authority. In the same way the usages which regulate the part played by the President and the Senate respectively in appointments to office are best justified on the ground that they make for the avoidance of disturbance and confusion. It would have been fatal to the peace of the country if President and Senate had severally stood on the letter of their rights and insisted on exercising powers that each might technically have claimed. The smooth working of the machinery of government could only be secured by the frank acceptance of a policy of give and take. The solution of such a problem usually involves the surrender, by a public body or a public officer, of certain powers which might legally be asserted—a surrender made, perhaps, in the first instance reluctantly and under pressure, but ultimately accepted as a normal and permanent condition of good government.

Further, the general tendency of the body of usage that has grown up has been in the direction of a greater and more direct popular control of the government. The net result has been to make the American political system more democratic than it was at the beginning or than it was originally intended or expected to be. The leading example is, of course, the revolutionary change made in the system of electing the President—both in the restriction of the

INDIRECT ELECTION

choice of Presidential Electors to the method of popular vote and in the forfeiture by the Electors themselves of the power to do anything more than register the popular will. Here the process has not been one of give and take. The Electors have had to give without taking. Their surrender has been brought about by the public demand for control without the receipt of any compensation for the sacrifice. The same principle is seen at work in the progress that was being made toward the establishment of a similar usage with respect to the election of Senators by the State Legislatures. It may be suggested, in passing, that what has happened in the United States deserves the careful attention of those who advocate the reform of the House of Lords by the introduction of a method of indirect election —an expedient which looks attractive but which is apt, under certain conditions, to be disappointing in actual operation. Mr. Freeman notes that there was nothing absurd, on the face of it, in the expectation that the system of Presidential Electors would be a reality ; that the primary electors would choose those men to whom they could best confide so great a trust, and that the Electors thus chosen would elect independently and fearlessly.

' It is the system,' he points out, ' adopted in the election of the legislature under the highly democratic constitution of Norway. But in Norway there are no political parties answering to those of England and America . . . Such an intermediate body becomes a farce in any country where there are strongly marked political parties.' [1]

[1] E. A. Freeman, *Historical Essays*, first series, 5th ed. p. 404.

Whether the method now established by usage is actually more democratic than that which it supplanted may be open to question. There are some American writers who doubt whether, after all, it is not the form rather than the substance of democratic control that the people have gained by the change. But the point relevant to our present study is that the change, whether it has answered its intention or not, was brought about by the pressure of the democratic spirit and in the belief that it would broaden the basis of the national government and make the choice of its Chief Executive a direct expression of the popular will.

XII

THE 'SAFEGUARDS' OF THE AMERICAN CONSTITUTION

THERE seems no utilitarian end to be served by attempting to classify Constitutions. It is not as though they were articles imported into a country under a tariff and therefore liable to varying rates of duty according to their conformity to the categories of a protective schedule. But there is a certain impulse in the order-loving mind which will not be denied the opportunity of ranging them in separate groups. The conventional distinction between Written and Unwritten Constitutions has been discussed in the introduction to this book. In place of it Lord Bryce has suggested, in his chapter on the subject in his *Studies in History and Jurisprudence*, a differentiation between Flexible and Rigid Constitutions. With all respect to so eminent an authority, one feels that he must surely have been nodding heavily when he made this proposal.

In the first place, the terms he suggests do not really indicate the distinction he has in mind. A flexible pen we know, and a flexible cane, and a flexible voice, and a flexible politician, and a flexible conscience, but a flexible Constitution—what can that be? Is it one which is sometimes stretched taut and sometimes relaxed, according to the mood of its custodians and interpreters? Is it a Constitution that is one thing 'between friends' and another thing between strangers? Such pliability must have been far from the intentions of the framers of any Constitution, and it is surprising to find it suggested as a basis of classification. Evidently what Lord Bryce is actually thinking of is the distinction not between flexibility and rigidity but between mutability and immutability—or, rather, since there does not exist, and has not existed since the days of the Medes and Persians, a political system which is absolutely unchangeable in any circumstances, between a greater and a lesser facility of change. It is certainly possible to grade Constitutions according as the process of amending them is easy or difficult. But, even so, this principle of classification is unsatisfactory because it is based on accidentals rather than essentials. It distorts one's whole perspective, tending, as it does, to lay the chief stress upon a feature that is really secondary. In grouping the Churches of Christendom according to their ecclesiastical systems or confessions of faith we should never think of making our classification according to the facility with which these systems or creeds may be modified, and it is no more reasonable to adopt such a dividing line in our grouping of systems of secular government. If we must classify political Constitutions, it would seem more helpful to pay attention especially to their content or *ethos*—to separate between the liberal and the conservative, the democratic and the aristocratic, and so on.

FACILITY OF CHANGE

However that may be, it is pertinent to consider whether the American Constitution is difficult or easy to change. If we were to adopt the basis of classification that Lord Bryce had in mind, should we find it inclining to the mutable or the immutable side? The answer to this question must obviously be affected by the view we take as to what the American Constitution really includes. The comparisons usually instituted between the American and other Constitutions, with respect to their mutability as well as their other qualities, treat the American Constitution as consisting of the Fundamental Law only, and contrast it with foreign Constitutions which are composed of statute law, common law, and usages. If, however, as has been contended in the introduction, these three elements help to make up the American Constitution also, our ultimate conclusion as to its ease or difficulty of alteration is likely to be somewhat different from the conclusion we should reach if we ignored everything in the American system except the Fundamental Law.

The Fundamental Law of the American Constitution is generally conceived of as both hard to change in itself and as interposing an impenetrable shield against hasty and ill-considered legislation by Congress.

'It is a noteworthy fact,' remarks Mr. Woodrow Wilson, ' that the admiration for our institutions which has during the past few years grown to large proportions among publicists abroad is almost all of it directed to the restraints we have effected upon the action of government.... It is always the static, never the dynamic, forces of our government which are praised.'[1]

This admiration for the safe and sane conservatism of the American system is most keenly felt in England at times when ancient institutions, especially those embodying the ' rights of property,' appear to be threatened by radical innovations. It found loud expression during the controversies of the early eighties respecting the extension of the franchise, and it is sure to be revived as soon as there comes into power a Labour Government backed by a parliamentary majority sufficient to carry through a Labour Party programme. Listen to Mr. Lecky as he laments English reluctance to follow the American example. It is ' absolutely essential,' he warns us, to the ' safe working ' of democracy

> ' that there should be a written Constitution, securing property and contract, placing serious obstacles in the way of organic changes, restricting the power of majorities, and preventing outbursts of mere temporary discontent and mere casual coalitions from overthrowing the main pillars of the State. In America such safeguards are largely and skilfully provided, and to this fact America mainly owes her stability. Unfortunately, in England men who are doing most to plunge the country into democracy are also the bitter enemies of all these safeguards, by which alone a democratic government can be permanently maintained.'[2]

[1] W. Wilson, *An Old Master and other Political Essays*, ed. 1893, p. 135.
[2] W. E. H. Lecky, *Democracy and Liberty*, ed. 1900, vol. i. p. 136.

Again, after discussing certain instances of corruption in the American government, he remarks that these things would not be acquiesced in

'were it not that an admirable written Constitution, enforced by a powerful and vigilant Supreme Court, had restricted to small limits the possibilities of misgovernment. All the rights that men value the most are placed beyond the reach of a tyrannical majority. . . . All the main articles of what British statesmen would regard as necessary liberties are guaranteed, and property is so fenced round by constitutional provisions that confiscatory legislation becomes almost impossible.'[1]

So, too, Sir Henry Maine, writing in his *Popular Government* just after the acute conflict of 1884, urges that Great Britain should ' borrow a few of the American securities against surprise and irreflection in constitutional legislation and express them with something like American precision.' He proposes that we should (1) make a distinction between ordinary legislation and legislation which in any other country would be called constitutional, and should (2) require for the latter a special legislative procedure, intended to secure caution and deliberation and as near an approach to impartiality as a system of party government will admit of.

The advantage of ' stability ' is thus conceived to be insured to the government of the United States by the necessity that every statute shall be consistent with the Fundamental Law of the Constitution, which is itself placed beyond possibility of easy change. There is a choice between two alternative

[1] *Op. cit.* vol. i. p. 116.

218 'SAFEGUARDS' OF CONSTITUTION

methods both of proposing amendments and of ratifying them. (1) ' The Congress, whenever two-thirds of both Houses shall deem it necessary, shall propose amendments to this Constitution, or (2) on the application of the Legislatures of two-thirds of the several States, shall call a convention for proposing amendments.' Whether the first or the second of these plans is adopted, the amendments thus proposed become part of the Fundamental Law ' when ratified (1) by the Legislatures of three-fourths of the several States or (2) by conventions in three-fourths thereof, as the one or the other mode of ratification may be proposed by the Congress.' Actually every amendment hitherto adopted has originated in Congress and has been ratified by the necessary majority of State Legislatures. The convention method has never been employed either for proposing amendments or for ratifying them.

The original document drawn up in 1787 has so far been modified by nineteen amendments. Ten of them, composing the so-called Bill of Rights, were ratified in 1791. The eleventh amendment dates from 1798 and the twelfth from 1804. More than half a century passed without any further change. Then came, between 1865 and 1870, a group of three amendments resulting from the Civil War. There followed another blank period until 1913, when the adoption of the sixteenth amendment broke the spell of silence, and stimulated the propaganda which led to the adoption of the seventeenth, eighteenth and nineteenth amendments.

THE PROCESS OF AMENDMENT

The belief that the process of amendment is exceptionally difficult is largely due to the impression made upon the public mind by the two long intervals of sixty-one and forty-three years respectively, during which the Fundamental Law remained unaltered. Indeed, between 1804 and 1913 the only changes effected were brought about after a way had been prepared for the constitutional method of amendment by the surgical operation of a four years' war. No wonder, then, that in the closing years of the nineteenth century and the early years of the twentieth it had almost become an accepted doctrine that the Fundamental Law of the American Constitution was practically beyond reach of change. But this conclusion was unwarranted, as the recent history of the Constitution shows. The fact that a thing has not been done is no proof that it is difficult to do, much less that it is impossible. The true explanation is doubtless that given by Dr. Nicholas Murray Butler in an address delivered in 1912, shortly before the revival of the amending process confirmed his diagnosis.

' The Constitution,' he said, ' is readily amendable whenever a large body of opinion, widely distributed throughout the country, genuinely desires its amendment. ... By far the greater part of the hundreds of amendments that have been proposed from time to time, some of which have received a considerable measure of support, have failed to secure incorporation in the Fundamental Law because the great mass of the American people were not interested in them or did not believe them to be important.' [1]

[1] N. M. Butler, *Is America Worth Saving?* ed. 1920, p. 158.

220 'SAFEGUARDS' OF CONSTITUTION

When we are considering the American practice as a possible example to other countries, we must not forget that the task of amending the Fundamental Law is made much more difficult than it would otherwise be owing to the complications of the Federal system. The need of the ratification of a proposed amendment by a large number of other Legislatures in addition to its approval by the national Congress is a mere corollary of the fact that America is a Federal Union of States. This requirement, which has naturally become more difficult to meet in proportion as the number of States has increased, has contributed largely to the delay in the adoption of amendments. If an attempt were made to copy the American practice elsewhere, there could be no parallel to this requirement except in countries which have likewise adopted a Federal system of government. In the United Kingdom, for instance, the nearest approach to it would be a provision requiring an Act of the Imperial Parliament which dealt with certain reserved subjects to be ratified by Provincial Parliaments of England, Scotland and Wales (or, rather, by two out of three of them) or by a three-fourths majority of the members of Parliament from each section.

When we are invited, as we so often are, to contrast the ease of constitutional change in England with its difficulty in America, on the ground that in England the most revolutionary change may be brought about by ' a mere Act of Parliament,' whereas in America the Fundamental Law is unalterable except by a

ANGLO-AMERICAN COMPARISONS

long process, it is necessary to point out that—except for the ratification provision, which is a corollary of the Federal system—the obstacle to radical change in America is, after all, scarcely greater than in England. The one difference between the two countries is the requirement in America that a two-thirds majority in Congress shall approve the change, whereas in England a bare majority in Parliament suffices. But the approval of Congress may be given in the form of a simple resolution, carried on a single division, without the three readings and committee stages that are needed to turn an English bill into an Act of Parliament, and without being exposed, like an American bill, to the risk of a veto by the President. No plebiscite is taken in America any more than in England. Even the ratification required is by State Legislatures which are bodies elected on the same franchise as Congress itself. It might, indeed, be contended with good reason that the existence of the House of Lords, which is not an elected body like the Senate of the United States, interposes a greater obstacle to constitutional change than the method prescribed by the American Fundamental Law for its own amendment. The Parliament Act, with its provision that no bill can become law without the consent of the Lords until it has been passed by the House of Commons in three successive sessions and that two years must have elapsed between the first reading in the first of these sessions and the final reading in the third, is really quite as effective a safeguard against gusts of popular sentiment as the alleged safeguards inherent in the American Fundamental Law. It is appropriate to quote here some wise words of Woodrow Wilson's:

> 'It is the habit,' he says, 'both of English and American writers to speak of the Constitution of Great Britain as if it were "writ in water," because nothing but the will of Parliament stands between it and revolutionary change. But is there nothing back of the will of Parliament? Parliament dare not go faster than the public thought. There are vast barriers of conservative public opinion to be overrun before a ruinous speed in revolutionary change can be attained. In the last analysis, our own Constitution has no better safeguard.'[1]

So much for the protection of the Fundamental Law against hasty change by formal amendment. We have now to consider how far its unique authority is a safeguard for those institutions and rights which are supposed to depend for their security upon the shield it interposes against the demagogue and the spoiler. Is there no way of getting round it? Listen to Mr. Chauncey Depew:

> 'If one of the framers of the Constitution could be reincarnated and visit us to-day, he would find the same great instrument almost unchanged, still the fundamental law of the land, but he would discover that legislation forced by the growth of the country, the rapid development of its resources, the influence of steam and electricity, had compelled the enactment of restrictive laws which he would regard as tyrannical restrictions upon individual liberty, and that those laws had been sustained as consti-

[1] W. Wilson, *An Old Master and other Political Essays*, ed. 1893, p. 149.

METHODS OF EVASION 223

tutional by the interpretations of the Supreme Court. He would discover that these interpretations had so treated the general principles of his Constitution as to make them applicable and serviceable for a process so radical as to seem to him revolutionary.'[1]

This utterance by a conservative may be supplemented by one from a radical:

'Actually,' says Mr. Walter E. Weyl, ' our Constitution is amended to-day (as it has been amended for the last 120 years) chiefly by process of interpretation. New senses are given to old words; the growing political foot, by sheer pressure, changes the old stiff shoe.'[2]

And Lord Bryce speaks of the expedient ' which is euphemistically called Extensive Interpretation, but may really amount to Evasion.'[3] So there are other means of releasing oneself from the inconvenient restraints of the Fundamental Law besides directing against it the frontal attack of a formal amendment.

That the interpretation of the text of an authoritative document is a fine art has been illustrated quite as notably in the constructions placed upon the Fundamental Law by the Supreme Court as in those placed upon any theological creed by any ecclesiastical assembly—or, for that matter, by any individual subscriber thereto. No doctrinal confession in the history of the Church has suffered a

[1] Chauncey M. Depew, in a speech delivered at Brooklyn on April 29, 1911, and published in *Speeches and Addresses on the Threshold of Eighty*, p. 11.
[2] Walter E. Weyl, *The New Democracy*, ed. 1912, p. 109.
[3] Lord Bryce, *Studies in History and Jurisprudence*, p. 194.

more startling metamorphosis in meaning, combined with an unimpaired respect for the letter, than the Fundamental Law of the American Constitution. It is not a coach and four but a heavily loaded freight train that has been driven through some of its clauses. According to Professor Goodnow

> 'the great increase in the action of the central government of the United States is due to the interpretation given by Congress and upheld by the Supreme Court to a number of powers granted to Congress in rather general terms by the Constitution.'[1]

The most important of these is the so-called 'commerce clause,' which authorizes Congress 'to regulate commerce with foreign nations and among the several States and with the Indian tribes.' By 'commerce' the framers of the Fundamental Law meant the carriage (or, as it is called in America, the 'transportation') of goods. But this clause, which was little utilized for a hundred years, has been held by the Supreme Court to justify not only the Sherman Act and other anti-trust legislation but even an Act for the suppression of lotteries. Viscount Grey has recently told us in his reminiscences that he once heard Mr. Roosevelt asked whether it would be possible in the United States to pass into law a budget with the changes in taxation corresponding to those proposed in Mr. Lloyd George's budget of 1909. The answer was not a learned exposition of the limitations of the American Constitution. It was simply this: 'It

[1] F. J. Goodnow, *Principles of Constitutional Government*, p. 44.

DISCREET NOMENCLATURE 225

would depend upon whether a Judge of the Supreme Court came down heads or tails.' But the effect of judicial interpretation in twisting the Fundamental Law from its original intent—or, if you prefer to put it so, in adapting it to new conditions—is so generally recognized that no more need be said about it here. Professor J. A. Jameson has spoken of 'unwritten Constitutions' as 'the playthings of judicial tribunals.'[1] This would be an apt description also of the fate of the Fundamental Law of the American Constitution, if we may trust the comments of many American writers of repute on the decisions of the Supreme Court.

A liberal construction of its text is only one of several methods of evading the Fundamental Law. One type of evasion might, perhaps, be called Evasion by Discreet Nomenclature. When is a treaty not a treaty? When it is an 'agreement' or a 'convention.' The Fundamental Law places the treaty-making power in the hands of the President 'by and with the advice and consent of the Senate, provided two-thirds of the Senators present concur.' But there have been many instances in which a President has made an arrangement with foreign powers which to all intents and purposes has been a treaty, but which, by being labelled an 'executive agreement,' has escaped being sent to the Senate for confirmation.[2] In one case, at least—that of

---

[1] J. A. Jameson, *A Treatise on Constitutional Conventions*, ed. 1887, p. 78.
[2] For examples see Senator S. M. Cullom, *Fifty Years of Public Service*, ed. 1911, pp. 393-5, and C. A. Beard, *American Government and Politics*, ed. 1924, pp. 204-205.

H.A.C.

President Roosevelt's Santo Domingo policy—a President submitted a treaty to the Senate, saw it rejected by that body, and then carried it into effect by concluding with the foreign government concerned an executive agreement in which were incorporated the principal terms of the rejected treaty. An even more startling example is the secret arrangement made by the same President with Japan in 1905 and revealed by Mr. Tyler Dennett in an address to the Williamstown Institute of Politics in August 7, 1924. In this address, and in his subsequent book on *Roosevelt and the Russo-Japanese War*, Mr. Dennett describes this agreement as virtually making the United States, for the period of the Roosevelt Administration, a member of the Anglo-Japanese Alliance. According to a document found among Mr. Roosevelt's papers after his death there was held on July 29, 1905, a conversation between Count Katsura, the Japanese Premier and Foreign Minister, and a personal representative of the President. Japan, said the Count, had a strong desire for an agreement with Great Britain and the United States to promote peace in the Far East. He knew the impossibility of a formal alliance with the United States, but he saw no obstacle to ' some good understanding for an alliance in practice if not in name.' The Roosevelt representative replied that while ' an understanding amounting in effect to a confidential informal agreement ' was impossible without the consent of the Senate, he felt sure that, when the occasion arose, ' appropriate action of the

TREATY MAKING

Government of the United States, in conjunction with Japan and Great Britain, for such a purpose could be counted on by them quite as confidently as if the United States were under treaty obligations ' to take it. The correct technical name for such a document, it appears, is an ' agreed memorandum.' A ' gentleman's agreement ' is the proper term for the arrangement with Japan, never submitted to the Senate for ratification, which regulated immigration from that country from 1908 to 1924. So, too, ' postal arrangements in the nature of treaties,'[1] as Mr. Taft calls them, have constantly been made with foreign countries without submission to the Senate. The ' face ' of the Senate—and of the Fundamental Law—is saved by calling them ' conventions.'

The Fundamental Law, again, contains an explicit provision that

> ' every order, resolution, or vote to which the concurrence of the Senate and the House of Representatives may be necessary (except on a question of adjournment) shall be presented to the President of the United States ; and before the same shall take effect, shall be approved by him, or, being disapproved by him, shall be repassed by two-thirds of the Senate and House of Representatives, according to the rules and limitations prescribed in the case of a bill.'

The technical name for a resolution of this kind is a ' joint resolution,' and its prescribed wording is ' Resolved, by the Senate and House of Representatives of the United States of America in Congress

[1] W. H. Taft, *Our Chief Magistrate and his Powers*, ed. 1916, p. 135.

assembled, that,' etc. It would seem impossible to evade such a plain instruction, but Congress has sought out many inventions and it has discovered one that answers the purpose here. Observe the ingenuity of the parliamentary juggler. Suppose you frame your resolution thus : ' Resolved, by the House of Representatives (the Senate concurring) that,' etc., or ' Resolved, by the Senate (the House of Representatives concurring) that,' etc. Then it becomes not a ' joint resolution ' but a ' concurrent resolution,' and may be put into effect without being submitted to the President at all.

Another class of evasions is made possible by the fact that no law—not even a Fundamental Law—comes into operation automatically. It requires some machinery to set it in motion.

> ' The Congress, by refusing to act,' says Mr. Alfred Pearce Dennis, ' can virtually nullify provisions of the organic law. For example, the Congress has never provided adequate machinery for enforcing the extradition clause of the Constitution. Governor Durbin, of Indiana, has steadily refused to surrender ex-Governor Taylor, indicted by a Kentucky court for complicity in the Goebel assassination. The Constitution provides that the governor of the asylum State shall " deliver up the fugitive on demand," but the Governor of Indiana pays no attention to the demand of Governor Beckham of Kentucky, and the Congress has provided no means for the execution of the constitutional mandate. It is possible, therefore, for a State governor to set himself up as a trial court, and arbitrarily refuse to surrender a fugitive from justice. Again, the provisions of the Fourteenth Amendment,

THE RIGHT TO VOTE

penalizing by a proportional reduction in representation any State which excludes from the suffrage adult male citizens, is to-day as worthless as a counterfeit note drawn on a broken bank. The constitutional provision appears to be automatic, but no legal provision is self-executing unless the government provides the means. Again and again the Congress has refused to take affirmative action in support of the constitutional mandate.'[1]

The scandal of the omission last mentioned deserves special attention if one would understand how far the specification of a civic right in the Fundamental Law is a guarantee of its preservation. The Fifteenth Amendment, whose adoption was one of the results of the Civil War, provides that ' the right of citizens of the United States to vote shall not be denied or abridged by the United States or by any State on account of race, colour, or previous condition of servitude.' That provision is to-day everywhere carried out to the letter. No negro is denied the vote because he is a negro. But there is nothing in this clause to prevent a State from imposing, let us say, an educational qualification on voters. For instance, it may require an applicant for registration as a voter to be able to read any section of the State Constitution or to understand it when read to him and give a reasonable interpretation thereof. A white man comes up to the clerk's desk and is tested by a passage so simple that it would be within the comprehension of a child. A coloured drayman or cotton-picker next presents himself and

[1] A. P. Dennis, in the *Atlantic Monthly*, October, 1905, p. 529.

the official reads to him: 'The State Legislature shall pass no bill of attainder or *ex post facto* law.' 'What,' he asks, 'do you understand by that?' The bewildered coloured man understands nothing by it, and is therefore deemed unfit to exercise the franchise. Variants of this device are employed in many of the Southern States, with the result that a network of barbed-wire entanglements obstructs the road of the coloured citizen to the polling booth.

There is apparently no means of preventing evasions of this kind, which are obviously quite compatible with an exact observance of the letter of the Fundamental Law. But, if the Fourteenth Amendment were carried out as it should be, a penalty, though a mild one, would be inflicted on States which practise them. This amendment, another of the national gains purchased at the cost of thousands of lives in the Civil War, provides that ' Representatives [*i.e.* to Congress] shall be apportioned among the several States according to their respective numbers, counting the whole number of persons in each State, excluding Indians not taxed. But when the right to vote at any election for the choice of Electors for President and Vice-President of the United States, Representatives in Congress, the executive and judicial officers of a State, or the members of the Legislature thereof, is denied to any of the male inhabitants of such State, being twenty-one years of age and citizens of the United States, or in any way abridged, except for participation in rebellion or other crime, the basis of repre-

AMENDMENT XIV

sentation therein shall be reduced in the proportion which the number of such male citizens shall bear to the whole number of male citizens twenty-one years of age in such State.' But the apportionment of Representatives is a task committed to Congress itself, and Congress has carefully refrained from attempting to carry out the instructions of the Fundamental Law in this respect. This clause of the Fourteenth Amendment is, in consequence, a dead letter. It should be noted that the States which virtually disfranchise the negro would not be the only ones to be affected by the enforcement of this provision. ' Massachusetts with an educational test, or Pennsylvania with a tax qualification,' says Dr. C. A. Beard, ' is legally quite as liable to a reduction of representation as any Southern State with a property or literacy qualification in its constitution.'[1]

Recent history supplies a glaring example of the ignoring not of an amendment to the Fundamental Law but of one of its original provisions. The second section of the very first article of that document requires the apportionment of representatives in Congress among the several States to be based upon their population, according to a census to be taken every ten years. Yet representation in the Congress elected in November, 1924, was determined by the figures of the census not of 1920 but of 1910. During the decade between these two enumerations there took place the greatest shift of population from

[1] C. A. Beard, *American Government and Politics*, ed. 1924, p. 124.

rural to urban districts in all the history of the United States, the percentage of urban population increasing from 45.8 to 51.4. The neglect of Congress to carry out the duty of revising its own composition has therefore resulted in giving the rural districts more weight than they are entitled to and the urban districts less—a situation which, as some protesting American journals have pointed out, tends toward the 'rotten borough' system.

How easily a provision of the Fundamental Law might be nullified by sheer inadvertence was illustrated by an amusing incident that occurred when President Taft was forming his administration. Shortly after the appointment of Senator Knox as Secretary of State had been announced, a Washington journalist happened to be calling at a government office for an interview. To pass away the time of waiting until the official was free to see him, he took up a copy of the Fundamental Law that was lying on a table in the ante-room. Glancing idly through its pages he lighted upon this article: 'No Senator or Representative shall, during the time for which he was elected, be appointed to any civil office under the authority of the United States, which shall have been created or the emoluments whereof shall have been increased during such time.' It suddenly flashed upon him that Mr. Knox was accordingly disqualified for Cabinet office, for when he had accepted the appointment he had not completed the term for which he was elected to the Senate, and during that period a law had been passed increasing

KNOX RELIEF ACT 233

the salaries of Cabinet officers. The discovery was, of course, excellent 'copy' for the newspaper to which this journalist was attached, and it created temporary consternation in the highest circles. The only way out was the passing of a measure, popularly known as the Knox Relief Act, which put the salary of the Secretary of the State back to the figure at which it had previously stood. Mr. Knox himself was an eminent constitutional lawyer. The President who made the appointment was a former Judge of a Federal Court, and among Mr. Knox's colleagues in the new Cabinet were several other distinguished members of the Bar, including, of course, the Attorney-General. Yet not one of them, however familiar with those provisions of the Fundamental Law which affect everyday affairs, had remembered this pertinent article. The imminent breach of it was prevented by the merest accident.

' But,' some one may naturally ask, ' what is the Supreme Court doing all this time? Where is the "powerful and vigilant" tribunal by whose watchful care, according to Mr. Lecky, the "admirable written Constitution" is "enforced"?' The supposed vigilance of the Supreme Court is an illusion. For the Court is a sentinel who never issues a challenge unless some one calls his attention to the fact that a stranger is passing who may reasonably be suspected of not having the password. It is not an inspectorate or a detective force. It is not commissioned to cast its eyes over the whole domain of American government for the purpose of noting illegalities. It is not even charged with the duty of calling attention to sins of omission or commission of which Congress may be guilty. The measures passed by that body do not come before it regularly for review. It does not begin to be concerned with any breach of the Fundamental Law until such breach is definitely and specifically alleged in a concrete case that comes before it for trial. Just as an English Court of Appeal has no concern with the validity of the by-laws of a railway company until a test case, brought by some aggrieved passenger, raises the question whether the company in making such and such a by-law was acting *ultra vires*, so the Supreme Court of the United States has no concern with the constitutionality of any statute until an act performed on the authority of that statute provokes a protest which leads to a judicial decision on the point. So that, if a statute is passed to which nobody objects, the question of its constitutionality never reaches the Court at all. The Court has no occasion for pronouncing any act of Congress invalid if it is unanimously supported by public opinion, or for condemning an official act in which there is unbroken acquiescence.

Even when a statute or an official practice is admittedly in conflict with the Fundamental Law it does not necessarily follow that the Supreme Court will pronounce it invalid. This statement will be such a shock to many readers that I hasten to add that my authority for it is the present Chief Justice of the United States. Mr. Taft, referring to the

LIBERTY IN WAR-TIME 235

remission of penalties incurred by steamers violating the navigation laws, says:

> 'Since the beginning of the government the Secretary of the Treasury has exercised the power to remit these penalties in proper cases. The pardoning power is given by the Constitution to the President, yet the practice of one hundred years was recognized by the Supreme Court, and it was held to be valid.'[1]

From another source one learns that this power was conferred on the Secretary of the Treasury by legislation, which was 'upheld by the Supreme Court in 1885, as justified by such a long practice and acquiescence as to amount to a settled interpretation of the Constitution.'[2]

If such exceptions can be allowed in time of peace, we know what to expect during war. *Inter arma silent leges*—even the Fundamental Law of the American Constitution. During both the American Civil War and the World War and during the period immediately following these wars, action was taken by the authorities again and again which was in direct violation of the Fundamental Law. The safeguards it provides for individual liberties—the 'citadels to make secure what your ancestors and ours had won,' as Mr. C. E. Hughes described them in his address to the English Bar in 1924—were virtually, though not avowedly, under a moratorium. Anyone who is interested in a study of the breaches of

[1] W. H. Taft, *Our Chief Magistrate and his Powers*, ed. 1916, p. 135.
[2] J. H. Finley and J. F. Sanderson, *The American Executive and Executive Methods*, ed. 1908, p. 86.

the Fundamental Law that were permitted during the Civil War will find an account of them in Jefferson Davis's history of *The Rise and Fall of the Confederate Government.* The story of similar violations of it during and after the World War is admirably summarized by Dr. C. A. Beard in the latest edition of his *American Government and Politics.* After his exposition of 'the grand principles of personal liberty set forth in the Constitution' Dr. Beard says that

> ' in actual practice, during American participation in the World War and for many months afterwards, Federal authorities played fast and loose with them—so fast and loose that a committee of eminent lawyers, among whom were two members of the Harvard Law School, was moved to make a public protest and file a list of violations of law committed by the government itself.'

He sums up as follows :

> ' It is conservative to say that the constitutional limitations on behalf of personal liberty proved no barrier to the Federal Government in arresting and imprisoning persons charged with holding objectionable opinions. The officers of the law had a practically free hand, and they were almost uniformly sustained by the courts of law.'[1]

In an address delivered in Washington on October 15, 1923, Senator Borah declared that in his opinion the First Amendment, which he regarded as ' the supreme test of a free government '—this is the Amendment which prohibits Congress from making any law ' abridging the freedom of speech or of the

[1] C. A. Beard, *American Government and Politics*, ed. 1924, pp. 108-11.

THE PRESIDENT AS AUTOCRAT 237

press or the right of the people peaceably to assemble and to petition the government for a redress of grievances '—had been ' disregarded and violated for six long years.' ' There are men in prison to-day,' he continued, ' not for the destruction of property, not for acts of violence, but because they were charged with expressing their political views upon political questions. But what is still more startling, they are there without any legal evidence sufficient to hold them. I have here upon my desk, but which I shall not take time to read, ample evidence of what I say to you.'[1]

Not only have individual rights been thus restricted unconstitutionally in war-time, but the emergency has been held to justify the exercise by the President of powers for which there is no warrant in the Fundamental Law. Dr. Lucius H. Holt, Professor of History at the United States Military Academy, West Point, thus summarizes what happened :

> ' In our own country, under the stress of the World War, the President asked and received from Congress the most extensive and autocratic powers of action. Not only is there no precedent in our own constitutional history for such powers as the President received by act of Congress, but it is undoubtedly true that these powers were themselves inconsistent with the provisions of the Constitution itself. In anything but a war emergency, the yielding of Congress of such powers to the President, and the acceptance by the President of such powers, would have been

[1] W. E. Borah, *American Problems*, ed. 1924, p. 313. For full particulars, see *Freedom of Speech*, by Zechariah Chafee, Jr., Professor of Law at Harvard.

instantly challenged by individuals of the state, and the question of constitutionality referred to the Supreme Court for a decision. During the war emergency, however, no such question was raised.'[1]

Lastly, if the Fundamental Law has not been formally amended, or made by the process of judicial interpretation to bear a meaning entirely alien from the intention of its framers, or evaded by an ingenious juggling with names, or nullified by the indifference of Congress to its clear instructions, it may still be radically changed by the growth of usages which become as firmly established, in actual practice, as any of its own provisions. *Littera scripta manet*, no doubt—but it may be overlaid nevertheless by the palimpsest of usage.

' It is at once curious and instructive,' remarks Mr. Woodrow Wilson in the chapter on the Executive in his *Congressional Government*, ' to note how we have been forced into practically amending the Constitution without constitutionally amending it. The legal processes of constitutional change are so slow and cumbersome that we have been constrained to adopt a serviceable framework of fictions which enables us easily to preserve the forms without laboriously obeying the spirit of the Constitution.... We have resorted, almost unconscious of the political significance of what we did, to extra-constitutional means of modifying the Federal system where it has proved to be too refined by balances of divided authority to suit practical uses.'

' Curious and instructive,' indeed, it is to read to-day some of the passages in Hamilton's exposition of the

[1] L. H. Holt, *The Elementary Principles of Government*, ed. 1923, p. 36.

Fundamental Law, and to observe how the safeguards he supposed it to provide have now disappeared. In No. 59 of the *Federalist* he is arguing that there is no danger of the government's being carried on for the advantage of special interests, and he supports his argument by pointing out that

> ' the House of Representatives being to be elected immediately by the people, the Senate by the State Legislatures, the President by Electors chosen for that purpose by the people, there would be little probability of a common interest to cement these different branches in a predilection for any particular class of electors.'

Again, in No. 63, he shows that, in the assignment of the treaty-making power to the President and the Senate conjointly, such precautions have been taken ' as will afford the highest security that it will be exercised by men the best qualified for the purpose and in the manner most conducive to the public good.' For the President is to be chosen by select bodies of Electors and the appointment of Senators has been committed to the State Legislatures.

> ' This mode,' Hamilton continues, ' has in such cases vastly the advantage of elections by the people in their collective capacity, where the activity of party zeal, taking advantage of the supineness, the ignorance and the hopes and fears of the unwary and interested, often places men in office by the votes of a small proportion of electors.'

Partly by formal amendment of the Fundamental Law and partly by the growth of usage, the guarantees on which Hamilton laid such stress have to-day ceased to exist.

'SAFEGUARDS' OF CONSTITUTION

It is remarkable that custom, which precedes formal law in regulating the life of primitive tribes, should be so potent in the political development of the latest civilizations. Indeed, Freeman has pointed out [1] that in England it was only after the supremacy of law had been firmly established by the Revolution of 1688 that most of our conventions of the Constitution were evolved.

> 'At no earlier time,' he says, 'have so many important changes in constitutional doctrine and practice won universal acceptance without being recorded in any written enactment.' 'The real difference,' he tells us, 'is that in more settled times, when law was fully supreme, it was found that many important practical changes might be made without formal changes in law. It was also found that there is a large class of political subjects which can be best dealt with in this way by tacit understandings and which can hardly be made the subjects of formal enactments by law.'

He gives as an example the convention that Ministers must resign when they cease to possess the confidence of the House of Commons, on which he comments that 'it would be utterly impossible to define such cases beforehand in terms of an Act of Parliament.' We can watch a precisely similar process at work in the United States, where many a defect that experience has revealed in the Fundamental Law has been corrected by the creation and crystallization of a usage. 'It may be asserted without much exaggeration,' declares Professor Dicey,

[1] E. A. Freeman, *The Growth of the English Constitution*, ed. 1887, p. 124.

'that the conventional element in the Constitution of the United States is now as large as in the English Constitution.'[1] And some of these usages are of the most radical nature, fully justifying Dr. C. A. Beard's statement that ' the most complete revolution in our political system has not been brought about by amendments or by statutes, but by the customs of political parties in operating the machinery of the government.'[2] In this way some of the most important provisions of the Fundamental Law have become to-day nothing more than legal fictions.

The change that has thus been wrought in the system of his own national government is little realized by the American citizen. Again and again the Fundamental Law has been nullified in practice by judicial interpretation, by sheer neglect to carry out its provisions, and by the accretion of usages which, even if they observe it in the letter, do violence to its intention and spirit. In short, the attempt to contrive what Mr. Walter Lippmann happily calls ' an automatic governor ' of the political machine has broken down. Yet it is still the orthodox and popular belief that the Fundamental Law of the American Constitution stands out unshaken like a Rock of Gibraltar in the midst of a changing world, and that nothing short of an earthquake could avail to disturb it. There appears periodically in

[1] A. V. Dicey, *Introduction to the Study of the Law of the Constitution*, ed. 1915, p. 28, footnote. It will be observed that in this passage Dicey regards the Constitution of the United States as not consisting of the Fundamental Law merely.

[2] C. A. Beard, *American Government and Politics*, ed. 1924, p. 96.

the American press a story of a mountain in Colorado which, from some cause hitherto undiscovered by geological science, every now and then shifts its position, sometimes to the extent of several feet a day, displacing the normal level of the roads and railways that communicate between the neighbouring towns. One may, perhaps, discern in this freak of nature some analogy to what has happened, and is still happening, in the political world. If the Fundamental Law is a rock, it is a moving rock. It would be strange, indeed, if the political system of the United States possessed a fixity beyond that of the political systems of other countries. For in America, more than anywhere else, what you see to-day is not unlikely to have disappeared by to-morrow. It seems only yesterday that the first skyscraper was erected, yet many examples of this new architectural device have already been 'scrapped.' An unchanging and unchangeable scheme of government would be in striking contrast with the rest of the national life, which is not set in moulds but is in a constant state of flux. One thing, and one only, seems to be beyond the reach of change, and that is the American citizen's conviction, amounting almost to a superstition, that a system of government devised by the Fathers of the Republic with well-nigh superhuman wisdom has been guaranteed to him and his heirs for ever by being inscribed in a 'written Constitution.' For him, surely, there is no need of the eternal vigilance required of less-favoured peoples. Have not his liberties and rights been enshrined, once for all, in a sacrosanct form of words, and placed safely beyond the grasp of devouring time?

The present Holy Trinity Church, Guildford, occupies the site of an earlier building, which was destroyed in 1740, when the steeple fell and carried the roof with it. One of the first persons to be informed of the disaster was the verger. 'It is impossible,' he exclaimed, 'for I have the key in my pocket.'

THE END

INDEX

Acton, Lord, on President's power of removal, 144 *n*; on residential qualification for Congress, 161.
Adams, John Quincy, Plumer's single vote for, 47; on Tyler's usurpation, 73.
Alaska, purchase of, 151.
Amendments, Constitutional, 13, 218; first, 236; twelfth, 29; fourteenth, 230; fifteenth, 229; seventeenth, 205; eighteenth, 13.
America, ambiguity of word, 16.
American Review of Reviews, quoted, 53 *n*.
Anson, Sir W. R., on residential qualification for Parliament, 169 *n*.
Appointment, powers of, 126.
Appropriation Bills, 154; riders to, 156.
Arthur, Chester A., on Presidential inability, 78.
Atlantic Monthly, quoted, 154 *n*, 229 *n*.
Attorney-General of U.S., 106, 139, 181.

Ballot, American use of word, 49; papers, form of, 38.
Bancroft, George, on third Presidential term, 98.
Beard, Charles A., on nature of American Constitution, 10; on economic factor in Fundamental Law, 27 *n*; on share of Congressmen in appointments, 129; on 'tacking,' 158; on qualifications for Congress, 168; on executive agreements, 225 *n*; on restrictions of franchise, 231; on liberty in war-time, 236; on effect of custom, 241.
Bigelow, John, on third Presidential terms, 91 *n*, 98 *n*.
Bishop, Joseph B., on Roosevelt's appointments to office, 134, 135 *n*.
Blaine, James G., and 1880 convention, 92.
Borah, William E., on Warren nomination, 140; on freedom of speech in war-time, 237.
Bosses, party control by, 49.
Bradford, Gamaliel, on third Presidential terms, 89, 93 : on Cabinet Ministers and Congress, 121, 123.
Bradley, Joseph P., on Presidential Electors, 41.
Bryce, Lord, on written *vs.* unwritten constitutions, 3 *n*; on Presidential Electors, 40; on third Presidential terms, 89; on 'tacking,' 158; on residential qualification for Congress, 171 *n*, 174; on Presidential messages, 198; on flexible *vs.* rigid constitutions, 213; on Extensive Interpretation, 223.
Burgess, John W., on Presidential Electors, 35; on Cabinet, 110; on Pres. Hayes' Cabinet nominations, 137 *n*; on 'tacking,' 158.
Burton, Theodore E., on strain upon Presidents, 85; and appointments to office, 130.

INDEX

Butler, Nicholas Murray, on failure of proposed amendments to Fundamental Law, 219.

Cabinet, during Pres. Wilson's illness, 81, 109; creation of, 101; relation to Congress, 113; President's freedom in forming, 136; removals from, 146; geographical distribution of seats in, 183; salaries of members, 232.
Caucus, nomination of President by Congressional, 43.
Chafee, Zechariah, Jr., on liberty in war-time, 237 n.
Charter, term suggested for Fundamental Law, 17.
Clark, Champ, and residential qualifications for Congress, 161, 162.
Cleveland, Frederick A., on restricted use of word 'constitution,' 11, 17.
Cleveland, Grover, on Presidential Electors, 28 n; and third Presidential terms, 92; in conflict with Senate, 145; absence from U.S. during term, 202.
Commerce Clause, 19, 224.
Concurrent Resolutions, 227.
Confederacy, Constitution of, 78, 121, 124, 144.
Congress, enactments declared unconstitutional by Supreme Court, 6, 178, 186, 233; caucus nominating Presidential candidates, 43; relations to Cabinet, 113; committees, 115, 119, 197; financial authority, 149; deficient in capable leaders, 167; public sessions, 175; 'joint' and 'concurrent' resolutions, 227. *See also* Representatives and Senate.
Congressional Globe, 72.
Congressional Record, 181 n.
Conkling, Roscoe, and 1880 convention, 92.
Constitutions, defined, 3; ambiguity in use of word, 15; classification of, 213; written *vs.* unwritten, 1, 10; flexible *vs.* rigid, 213.
Constitution, American, analysed, 5, 21; needs a Bagehot, 24; safeguards of, 212. *See also* Fundamental Law.
Constitution, English, analysed, 1, 3; contrasted with American, 1, 216, 220; development of conventions of, 240.
Convention of 1787, debates and decisions, 6, 13, 26, 30, 88, 102, 127, 152, 205.
Conventions of the Constitution, 4, 21.
Conventions, party, 46, 48, 92.
Cooley, Thomas M., defines a constitution, 4.
Coolidge, Calvin, becoming President, 58; attending Cabinet meetings while Vice-President, 112; and nominations to Cabinet, 137; and removals from Cabinet, 146.
Council of State, proposals for, 102.
Cox, James M., nominated for Presidency, 49.
Crandall, S. B., on Jay Treaty, 151 n.
Croly, Herbert, on Fundamental Law, 26; on Mark Hanna and appointments to office, 129, 132.
Cullom, Shelby M., on executive agreements, 225 n.
Curtis, George W., excluded from Congress, 162.

Davis, Jefferson, on Cabinet ministers and Congress, 124; on breaches of Fundamental Law during Civil War, 236.
Dawes, Charles G., on attendance of Vice-President at Cabinet meetings, 112.
Democracy, repugnant to founders of U.S., 26; usages of Constitution making for, 210.
Dennett, Tyler, on Roosevelt's arrangement with Japan, 226.

246 INDEX

Dennis, Alfred P., on nullification of Fundamental Law, 228.
Departments, Executive, 106, 119.
Depew, Chauncey M., on revolutionary changes in Fundamental Law, 222.
Dewitt, David M., on impeachment of Andrew Johnson, 75.
Dicey, Albert Venn, defines a constitution, 3; analyses English Constitution, 4; on Presidential Electors, 40; on conventions that have become laws, 203; on conventional element in American Constitution, 240.
Dougherty, J. H., on election of President, 28 *n*, 33 *n*.

Election, indirect, 28, 211.
Executive agreements, 225.
Executive sessions, 178.
Extradition, inter-State, 228.

Farrand, Max, on election of President by House of Representatives, 30; on meetings of Presidential electors, 41 *n*; on secrecy in Continental Congress, 176 *n*.
Federalist, quoted, 26, 31, 32, 102, 127, 143, 239.
Finance, control of national, 149.
Finley, John H., on exercise of pardoning power by Secretary of Treasury, 235 *n*.
Flexibility, as criterion in classifying constitutions, 213.
Foraker, Joseph B., on movement for third nomination of Grant, 92.
Ford, Henry J., on Cleveland's conflict with Senate, 146 *n*; on Congressmen and spoils, 164; otherwise quoted, 117 *n*, 121 *n*, 128 *n*.
Franchise, early limitations of, 27; educational qualifications for, 229.
Frank, Glenn, on Foreign Relations Committee of Senate, 168.

Freeman, Edward Augustus, on conventions of English Constitution, 7, 240; on third Presidential terms, 97; on Cabinet ministers and Congress, 118; on official titles, 193; on indirect elections, 211.
Fundamental Law, use of term, 19; interpreted by Supreme Court, 6, 185, 223, 234; supposed difficulty of changing, 215; amendment of, 218; does not work automatically, 228; violated during war, 235; radically changed by usage, 238; compared to Rock of Gibraltar, 241.
Fundamental Law, its provisions, (or lack of provisions) relating to election of President, 26; 'accidental' Presidents, 58; re-eligibility of President, 88; President's advisers, 101; relations of Federal office-holders to Congress, 113, 182; power of appointment, 126; power of removal, 142; control of national finances, 149, 152, 154; treaty-making power, 150, 225; qualifications for Congress, 160; public sessions of Congress, 175; geographical distribution of offices, 183; composition of Supreme Court, 187; titles of nobility and honour, 190; Presidential messages to Congress, 198; election of Senators, 203; joint resolutions, 227; limitations of franchise, 229; Congressional apportionment, 230, 231; increased salary of office-holders, 232.

Gallatin, Albert, debate on qualifications of, 176.
Garfield, James Abram, illness of, 78; in conflict with Senate, 145.
Gerrymander, utilized to exclude party leaders from Congress, 165.
Ghent, centenary of Treaty of, 202.

INDEX 247

Goodnow, Frank J., on interpretations of Fundamental Law by Supreme Court, 224.
Governors, British colonial, 67 ; American State, and extradition, 228.
Grant, Ulysses S., and third Presidential term, 91 ; withdraws Cabinet nomination, 136.
Greeley, Horace, death of, 51.
Grey, Viscount, not received by Pres. Wilson, 80 ; quoted, 224.

Hadley, Arthur T., on election of Senators, 204.
Hamilton, Alexander, and presentation of report to Congress, 114 ; on election of President, 31, 32 ; on proposals for Council of State, 102 ; on appointments to office, 127 ; on removals from office, 143 ; on safeguards of Fundamental Law, 238.
Hanna, Mark, and patronage, 129.
Harding, Warren Gamaliel, nomination of, 49 ; and formation of Cabinet, 109 ; invites Vice-President to Cabinet Meetings, 111.
Harrison, Benjamin, on Presidential Electors, 38 ; on appropriation bills, 155 ; on integrity of Supreme Court, 189.
Harrison, William Henry, death of, 69.
Hart, Albert Bushnell, on third Presidential terms, 88.
Haskin, Frederic J., quoted 202 n.
Hayes, Rutherford B., in conflict with Congress, 136, 157.
Hendrick, Burton J., quoted, 203 n.
Hoar, Roger S., *Constitutional Conventions*, 22.
Holmes, Oliver Wendell, on American appetite for titles, 191.
Holt, Lucius H., on Presidential autocracy in war-time, 237.
Honourable, prefix of, 192.
Hoover, Herbert C., as member of Cabinet, 109.

Hughes, Charles Evans, refuses to appear before Senate Committee, 115 ; on safeguards of individual liberties, 235.

Ingalls, Senator, on Presidential Electors, 41.
Interpretation, Extensive, 223.
Iredell, James, on requirement of written opinions from members of Cabinet, 103.

Jackson, Andrew, and third Presidential terms, 91 ; enlargement of Cabinet by, 106.
Jameson, J. Alexander, *Constitutional Conventions*, 21 ; on unwritten constitutions, 225.
Jameson, J. Franklin, on Presidential Electors, 41.
Japan, American relations with, 226.
Jay Treaty, 151, 178.
Jefferson, Thomas, and third Presidential terms, 91 ; and Louisiana purchase, 151 ; and messages to Congress, 198.
Johnson, Andrew, impeachment of, 75 ; in conflict with Congress, 144, 156, 188.
Joint Resolutions, 227.

King, Rufus, on meetings of Presidential Electors, 41 n.
Knights, American, 191.
Knox, Philander Chase, on absence of President from U.S., 201 ; Act passed for relief of, 233.

Lamont, Thomas W., on Pres. Wilson at Paris, 84 n.
Law, written vs. unwritten, 2.
Lawrence, David, on Pres. Wilson's illness, 80, 81, 82, 109 n ; on Pres. Wilson's desire for third term, 96 ; on Pres. Wilson's decision to read his message to Congress, 199 n.
Lawyers, in Congress, 171.
League of Nations, U.S. and, 81.

248 INDEX

Learned, Henry Barrett, on President's Cabinet, 102 n, 107, 111.
Lecky, W. E. H., on secret sessions of Senate, 179 n ; on safeguards of American political system, 216, 233.
Legal Tender Acts, 188.
Liberty, violated during and after war, 235.
Lieutenant-Governor, in British colonies, 67.
Lincoln, Abraham, and his Cabinet, 107.
Lippmann, Walter, on Congressional committees of investigation, 119 ; on an 'automatic governor' of political machine, 241.
Lodge, Henry Cabot, on antidemocratic character of Fundamental Law, 27 ; on visits of President to Senate, 104 ; on Senate and appointments, 131 ; on Senate and financial legislation, 153, 155.
Long, John D., on 'carrion' of patronage, 130.
Lowell, A. Lawrence, on changing conventions of English Constitution, 196.

M'Call, Samuel Walker, on revenue bills, 154 ; on T. B. Reed's first election to Congress, 164 n.
M'Clure, A. K., on methods of appointing Presidential Electors, 33 n ; on Tyler's assumption of Presidency, 69.
MacDonald, William, on proposals for associating Cabinet with Congress, 125 n.
M'Kinley, William, use of gerrymander against, 165.
Madison, James, on democracies, 26 ; on election of President, 31.
Maine, Sir H. J. S., on American 'securities against surprise and irreflection,' 217.
Marshall, Thomas Riley, on Presidential Electors, 41.

Merriam, Charles E., on jockeying between President and Senate, 134.
Messages, Presidential, 198, 207.
Miller, Samuel F., on Presidential Electors, 41.
Monroe, James, single vote cast against, 46.
Morgan, John T., on publication of secret debates, 180.
Morrison, William Ralls, use of gerrymander against, 165.

Negroes, excluded from franchise, 229.
New Republic, quoted, 137, 139, 172.
New York Tribune, quoted, 91 n.
Norway, indirect election successful in, 211.

Office, appointment to and removal from, 126 ; combination of Federal and State, 182 ; geographical distribution of, 183 ; name of, used as personal title, 192.
Ohio, gerrymandering in, 165.
Oregon, election laws of, 36.

Page, Walter Hines, suggests that President Wilson should visit England, 202.
Pardoning power, 235.
Parliament, Cabinet ministers once excluded from, 113 ; questions in, 116 ; former residential qualification for, 169 ; better reflex of national life than Congress, 171 ; safeguards against extravagance, 163.
Parliament Act, 221.
Parties, American, regulated by statute, 36.
Patronage, President's, 133.
Peary, Robert Edwin, rewarded for discoveries by rise in naval rank, 194.
Pennsylvania, election laws of, 36.
Platt, Orville H., on secrecy of Senate executive sessions, 181 n.

INDEX 249

Plumer, William, votes independently as Presidential Elector, 46.
Plumer, William, Jr., quoted, 47.
Polk, James Knox, and his Cabinet, 107.
President, method of electing, 26; method of nominating, 43; 'accidental,' 58; 'inability' of, 64, 77; absence from U.S. during term of office, 82, 201; duties of, 83; re-eligibility for second and third terms, 88; and Senate, 101, 126, 209, 239; and Cabinet, 101, 136, 146; powers of appointment and removal, 126; communicating messages to Congress, 198, 207; exercising autocratic power in wartime, 237. *See also* Presidential Electors.
Presidential Electors, 7, 8, 28, 204, 207, 211, 239.
Primaries, direct, 48.
Progressive Convention, 95.
Prohibition Amendment, 13.
Pulitzer, Joseph, in favour of indirect election to Presidency, 208.

Questions in Parliament, 116.

Redfield, William C., on strain upon President, 85; on election to Congress as financial prize, 173.
Reed, Thomas B., first election to Congress, 164, 173.
Regency, a parallel to Acting Presidency, 66.
Removal, President's vs. Senate's power of, 142.
Representatives, House of, election of President by, 29, 42; share in patronage, 129; financial authority, 149; influence in making treaties, 150; residential qualification for membership, 160; lawyers in, 171; membership of, a financial prize, 172. *See also* Congress.

Rogers, Lindsay, on proportion of lawyers in Congress, 172 *n.*
Roosevelt, Theodore, and third Presidential term, 93, 98; and appointments to office, 134; on decisions of Supreme Court, 224; evades treaty-making restrictions, 226.
Salmon, Lucy M., on President's power of removal, 143 *n.*
Sanderson, J. F., on exercise of pardoning power by Secretary of Treasury, 235 *n.*
Santo Domingo Treaty, 180, 226.
Savannah, appointment of naval officer at, 127.
Sectionalism, Washington's warning against, 183.
Sedgwick, A. D., on Presidential Electors, 41.
Seitz, Don Carlos, quoted, 208 *n.*
Senate, Presidency of, 62; and Versailles Treaty, 81; and President of U.S., 101, 126, 209, 239; share in patronage, 126; 'courtesy' of, 129; financial authority of, 152; quality of, 168; and public sessions, 176; direct vs. indirect election of, 203, 239. *See also* Congress.
Seymour, Charles, quoted, 84 *n.*
Sherman, James Schoolcraft, death of, 52.
Sherman, Roger, on popular incompetence for government, 26.
Sherman Act, 19.
Smith, Goldwin, on 'fatuous localism,' 162.
Smith, Herbert A., on Cabinet ministers and Legislatures, 122 *n.*
Sparks, Jared, on secret sessions of Continental Congress, 176 *n.*
Speaker of House of Representatives, 197.
Stanwood, Edward, on methods of appointing Presidential Electors, 33 *n*; on Roosevelt's refusal of third term nomination, 94.

State Legislatures, and appointment of Presidential Electors, 33; and election of Senate, 158.
Stealey, Orlando O., on secrecy of Senate executive sessions, 180.
Story, Joseph, on residential qualification for Parliament, 169 n.
Stubbs, William, on residential qualification for Parliament, 169 n.
Supreme Court, power to declare statutes unconstitutional, 6, 185, 233; geographical distribution of seats on, 183; independence of, 185; possibility of 'packing,' 187; 'extensive interpretation' by, 223.

Tacking, 156.
Taft, William Howard, nomination for Presidency, 94, 95; choice of holiday resorts, 202; on early limitations of franchise, 28 n; on President's power to dispense with Cabinet, 110, 111; on relation of Cabinet to Congress, 116, 121, 122; on financial powers of Congress, 149; on 'tacking,' 159; on reading of message to Congress by President, 200; on arrangements equivalent to treaties, 227; on exercise of pardoning power by Secretary of Treasury, 235.
Tariff Bills, Senate and, 153.
Tenure of Office Act, 144.
Thayer, James Bradley, on third Presidential terms, 89, 99.
Tiedeman, Christopher G., *The Unwritten Constitution of the U.S.*, 23.
Titles of nobility and honour, 190.
Treaties, influence of House of Representatives in making, 150; privately discussed in Senate, 178; joint power of President and Senate in making, 225; and executive agreements, 225.
Tyler, John, assumption of Presidency by, 69, 87.
Tyler, Lyon G., quoted, 74.

Vice-President, method of electing, 29; becoming President, 58; and Presidency of Senate, 62; attending Cabinet meetings, 107, 111, 112.
Von Holst, Hermann E., on Presidential Electors, 40, 51, 53; on Senate and appropriation bills, 155.

Walker, Senator, on Tyler's claim to Presidency, 72.
War, Fundamental Law disregarded during, 235.
Warren, Charles Beecher, nominated for Attorney-Generalship, 137, 181.
Washington, newspaper correspondents at, 110, 119.
Washington, George, re-election of, 89, 98; and Senate, 104, 127; and his Cabinet, 106; and Jay Treaty, 151; warns against sectionalism, 183; and absence of President from U.S., 201.
Watterson, Henry, fears lest Roosevelt become a Diaz, 98.
West, Henry Litchfield, on President's patronage, 133.
Weyl, Walter E., on anti-democratic character of Fundamental Law, 27; on interpretation of Fundamental Law, 223.
Willoughby, Westel W., on integrity of Supreme Court, 187.
Wilson, Woodrow, illness, 80; visit to Paris, 82, 202; desire for third term, 95; reads message to Congress in person, 199; on American constitutional system, 9; on anti-democratic character of Fundamental Law, 27; on Presidential Electors, 40; on Vice-President, 64; on relations of Cabinet to Congress, 117; on lack of leaders in Congress, 167; on quality of Senate, 168; on Supreme Court and Legal Tender Acts, 188; on integrity of Supreme Court, 189; on foreign admiration for

American conservatism, 215 ; on limitations of British Parliament, 222 ; on informal amendments of Constitution, 238.

Wise, H. A., on Tyler's claim to Presidency, 72.

Woodburn, James A., on unwritten constitution of U.S., 10 ; on Presidential Electors, 37 ; on third Presidential terms, 88 ; on President's relations to Cabinet, 106.

Young, James Rankin, and reports of Senate executive sessions, 180.

Young, James Thomas, on appointments to office, 135 ; on residential qualification for Congress, 174 n.